God, You are my God;
I eagerly seek You.
I thirst for You. . . .
My lips will glorify You
because Your faithful love
is better than life.

—

Psalm 63:1, 3 HCSB

99 RADICAL ANSWERS

TO QUESTIONS MEN ASK

The quoted ideas expressed in this book (but not Scripture verses) are not, in all cases, exact quotations, as some have been edited for clarity and brevity. In all cases, the author has attempted to maintain the speaker's original intent. In some cases, quoted material for this book was obtained from secondary sources, primarily print media. While every effort was made to ensure the accuracy of these sources, the accuracy cannot be guaranteed. For additions, deletions, corrections, or clarifications in future editions of this text, please write Freeman-Smith, LLC.

Scripture quotations are taken from:

The Holy Bible, King James Version (KJV)

The Holy Bible, New International Version (NIV) Copyright © 1973, 1978, 1984, by International Bible Society. Used by permission of Zondervan Publishing House. All rights reserved.

The Holy Bible, New King James Version (NKJV) Copyright © 1982 by Thomas Nelson, Inc. Used by permission.

Holy Bible, New Living Translation, (NLT) copyright © 1996. Used by permission of Tyndale House Publishers, Inc., Wheaton, Illinois 60189. All rights reserved.

The Message (MSG)- This edition issued by contractual arrangement with NavPress, a division of The Navigators, U.S.A. Originally published by NavPress in English as THE MESSAGE: The Bible in Contemporary Language copyright 2002-2003 by Eugene Peterson. All rights reserved.

New Century Version®. (NCV) Copyright © 1987, 1988, 1991 by Word Publishing, a division of Thomas Nelson, Inc. All rights reserved. Used by permission.

The New American Standard Bible®, (NASB) Copyright © 1960, 1962, 1963, 1968, 1971, 1972, 1973, 1975, 1977, 1995 by The Lockman Foundation. Used by permission.

The Holman Christian Standard Bible™ (HCSB) Copyright © 1999, 2000, 2001 by Holman Bible Publishers. Used by permission.

Cover Design by Kim Russell / Wahoo Designs
Page Layout by Bart Dawson

ISBN 978-1-60587-269-8

Printed in the United States of America

99
RADICAL
ANSWERS

Introduction

When you have questions, where do you turn for answers? If you're a wise man, you will turn, first and always, to God's Word for the answers to life's biggest questions. This book contains 99 questions—along with radical, life-altering answers—based upon truths contained in God's Holy Word.

Being a Christian man in today's world isn't easy. Your world is filled with distractions and temptations that were unknown to previous generations. And the world is changing so rapidly that, at times, it seems difficult to catch your breath and keep your balance.

In a rapidly changing world, God remains unchanged. In a society that is built upon the shifting sands of popular culture, God's laws remain constant. In a time of uncertainty and doubt, God's promises are sure and true. This text is intended to reassure you of the eternal promises that are found in God's Holy Word and of God's never-ending love for you. May these pages help you answer the most important questions you face, and may you, in turn, share your answers with the friends and family members whom God has seen fit to place along your path.

What does the Bible say about putting God first in my life?

The Radical Answer:

God's Word is clear: If you put Him first in every aspect of your life, you'll be blessed. But if you relegate God to a position of lesser importance, you'll distance yourself from His blessings.

Who's First?

The thing you should want most is God's kingdom and doing what God wants. Then all these other things you need will be given to you.

Matthew 6:33 NCV

As you think about the nature of your relationship with God, remember this: you will always have some type of relationship with Him—it is inevitable that your life must be lived in relationship to God. The question is not if you will have a relationship with Him; the burning question is whether or not that relationship will be one that seeks to honor Him.

Are you willing to place God first in your life? And, are you willing to welcome God's Son into your heart? Unless you can honestly answer these questions with a resounding yes, then your relationship with God isn't what it could be or should be. Thankfully, God is always available, He's always ready to forgive, and He's waiting to hear from you now. The rest, of course, is up to you.

God is able to do anything He pleases with one ordinary person fully consecrated to Him.

Henry Blackaby and Claude King

God calls us to be committed to Him, to be committed to making a difference, and to be committed to reconciliation.

Bill Hybels

God deserves first place in your life . . . and you deserve the experience of putting Him there.

Jim Gallery

A Prayer:

Dear Lord, today I will honor You with my thoughts, my actions, and my prayers. I will seek to please You, and I will strive to serve You. Your blessings are as limitless as Your love. And because I have been so richly blessed, I will worship You, Father, with thanksgiving in my heart and praise on my lips, this day and forever. Amen

As a busy man, I feel overwhelmed sometimes. What can I do?

The Radical Answer:

One way to battle the rigors of everyday life is to slow down long enough to count your blessings. And make no mistake: you have many, many blessings to count.

You Are Blessed

The Lord bless you and keep you; the Lord make His face shine upon you, and be gracious to you.

Numbers 6:24-25 NKJV

If you sat down and began counting your blessings, how long would it take? A very, very long time! Your blessings include life, freedom, family, friends, talents, and possessions, for starters. But, your greatest blessing—a gift that is yours for the asking—is God's gift of salvation through Christ Jesus.

Today, give thanks for your blessings by accepting them fully (with open arms) and by sharing them generously (with a thankful heart).

Billy Graham had this advice: "Think of the blessings we so easily take for granted: Life itself; preservation from danger; every bit of health we enjoy; every hour of liberty; the ability to see, to hear, to speak, to think, and to imagine all this comes from the hand of God." And that's sound advice for Christians—like you—who have been blessed beyond measure.

God is more anxious to bestow His blessings on us than we are to receive them.

St. Augustine

Blessings can either humble us and draw us closer to God or allow us to become full of pride and self-sufficiency.

Jim Cymbala

God's kindness is not like the sunset—brilliant in its intensity, but dying every second. God's generosity keeps coming and coming and coming.

Bill Hybels

A Prayer:

Today, Lord, I count my many blessings. You have cared for me, Lord, and I will give thanks and praise You always. Today, let me share Your gifts with others, just as You first shared them with me. Amen

Sometimes I feel like my strength is almost gone. What can I do about that?

The Radical Answer:

If you need strength, slow down, get more rest, engage in sensible exercise, and turn your troubles over to God . . . . but not necessarily in that order.

Need Strength?

Create in me a pure heart, O God, and renew a steadfast spirit within me. Do not cast me from your presence or take your Holy Spirit from me. Restore to me the joy of your salvation and grant me a willing spirit, to sustain me.

Psalm 51:10-12 NIV

God is a never-ending source of strength and courage if we call upon Him. When we are weary, He gives us strength. When we see no hope, God reminds us of His promises. When we grieve, God wipes away our tears.

Do you feel overwhelmed by today's responsibilities? Do you feel pressured by the ever-increasing demands of 21st-century life? Then turn your concerns and your prayers over to God. He knows your needs, and He has promised to meet those needs. Whatever your circumstances, God will protect you and care for you...if you let

Him. Invite Him into your heart and allow Him to renew your spirits. When you trust Him and Him alone, He will never fail you.

Walking with God leads to receiving his intimate counsel, and counseling leads to deep restoration.

John Eldredge

One reason so much American Christianity is a mile wide and an inch deep is that Christians are simply tired. Sometimes you need to kick back and rest for Jesus' sake.

Dennis Swanberg

There are two things we are called to do: we are to depend on His strength and be obedient to His Word. If we can't handle being dependent and obedient, we will never become the kind of people who have a heart for God.

Stuart Briscoe

A Prayer:

Dear Lord, sometimes the demands of the day leave me discouraged and frustrated. Renew my strength, Father, and give me patience and perspective. Today and every day, let me draw comfort and courage from Your promises, from Your love, and from Your Son. Amen

What does the Bible say about my daily devotional?

The Radical Answer:

Time and again, the Bible stresses the need to study God's Word every day, with no exceptions. If you make your morning devotional an ironclad habit, you'll be blessed.

Every Day with God

Morning by morning he wakens me and opens my understanding to his will. The Sovereign Lord has spoken to me, and I have listened.

Isaiah 50:4-5 NLT

Each new day is a gift from God, and if we are wise, we will spend a few quiet moments each morning thanking the Giver. Daily life is woven together with the threads of habit, and no habit is more important to our spiritual health than the discipline of daily prayer and devotion to the Creator.

When we begin each day with our heads bowed and hearts lifted, we remind ourselves of God's love, His protection, and His commandments. And if we are wise, we will align our priorities for the coming day with the teachings and commandments that God has given us through His Holy Word.

Are you seeking to change some aspect of your life? Do you seek to improve the condition of your spiritual or physical health? If so, ask for God's help and ask for it many times each day . . . starting with your morning devotional.

We must appropriate the tender mercy of God every day after conversion or problems quickly develop. We need his grace daily in order to live a righteous life.

Jim Cymbala

I suggest you discipline yourself to spend time daily in a systematic reading of God's Word. Make this "quiet time" a priority that nobody can change.

Warren Wiersbe

A person with no devotional life generally struggles with faith and obedience.

Charles Stanley

A Prayer:
Lord, help me to hear Your direction for my life in the quiet moments when I study Your Holy Word. And as I go about my daily activities, let everything that I say and do be pleasing to You. Amen

What does the Bible say about righteousness?

The Radical Answer:

Because God is just, He rewards righteousness just as surely as He punishes sin. Try as we might, we simply cannot escape the consequences of our actions. How we behave today has a direct impact on the rewards we will receive tomorrow. That's a lesson that we must teach our loved ones by our words and our actions, but not necessarily in that order.

Doing the Right Thing

Lead a tranquil and quiet life in all godliness and dignity.

1 Timothy 2:2 HCSB

How do we live a life that is "right with God"? By accepting God's Son and obeying His commandments. Accepting Christ is a decision that we make one time; following in His footsteps requires thousands of decisions each day.

Whose steps will you follow today? Will you honor God as you strive to follow His Son? Or will you join the lockstep legion that seeks to discover happiness and fulfillment through worldly means? If you are righteous and wise, you will follow Christ. You will follow Him today and every day. You will seek to walk in His footsteps without reservation or doubt. When you do so, you will be "right with God" precisely because you are walking aright with His only begotten Son.

The best evidence of our having the truth is our walking in the truth.

Matthew Henry

If we have the true love of God in our hearts, we will show it in our lives. We will not have to go up and down the earth proclaiming it. We will show it in everything we say or do.

D. L. Moody

We must appropriate the tender mercy of God every day after conversion, or problems quickly develop. We need his grace daily in order to live a righteous life.

Jim Cymbala

A Prayer:

Holy Father, let my thoughts and my deeds be pleasing to You. I thank You, Lord, for Jesus, the One who took away my sins. Today and every day, I will follow in His footsteps so that my life can be a living testimony to Your love, to Your forgiveness, and to Your Son. Amen

Sometimes I'm worried about the future. What does God's Word say about my future?

The Radical Answer:

If you're given your heart to Jesus, God's Word promises that your future is intensely bright. Of course, you and your loved ones may encounter adversity and pain, but your eternal destiny is secure.

Your Bright Future

What a God we have! And how fortunate we are to have him, this Father of our Master Jesus! Because Jesus was raised from the dead, we've been given a brand-new life and have everything to live for, including a future in heaven—and the future starts now!

1 Peter 1:3-4 MSG

How bright is your future? Well, if you're a faithful believer, God's plans for you are so bright that you'd better wear shades. But here's an important question: How bright do you believe your future to be? Are you expecting a terrific tomorrow, or are you dreading a terrible one? The answer you give will have a powerful impact on the way tomorrow turns out.

Do you trust in the ultimate goodness of God's plan for your life? Will you face tomorrow's challenges with optimism and hope? You should. After all, God created you for a very important reason: His reason. And you still have important work to do: His work.

Today, as you live in the present and look to the future, remember that God has an amazing plan for you. Act—and believe—accordingly.

Hoping for a good future without investing in today is like a farmer waiting for a crop without ever planting any seed.

John Maxwell

The pages of your past cannot be rewritten, but the pages of your tomorrows are blank.

Zig Ziglar

The Christian believes in a fabulous future.

Billy Graham

A Prayer:

Dear Lord, as I look to the future, I will place my trust in You. If I become discouraged, I will turn to You. If I am afraid, I will seek strength in You. You are my Father, and I will place my hope, my trust, and my faith in You. Amen

What does the Bible say about the search for purpose and meaning?

The Radical Answer:

God has a wonderful plan for you and your family. Discovering God's purpose requires a willingness to be open. God's plan is unfolding day by day. If you keep your eyes and your heart open, He'll reveal His plans. God has big things in store for you, but He may have quite a few lessons to teach you before you are fully prepared to do His will and fulfill His purposes.

The Search for Purpose

For everything, absolutely everything, above and below, visible and invisible, rank after rank after rank of angels—everything got started in him and finds its purpose in him.

Colossians 1:16 MSG

Life is best lived on purpose. And purpose, like everything else in the universe, begins with God. Whether you realize it or not, God has a plan for your life, a divine calling, a direction in which He is leading you. When you welcome God into your heart and establish a genuine relationship with Him, He will begin, in time, to make His purposes known.

Sometimes, God's intentions will be clear to you; other times, God's plan will seem uncertain at best. But even on those difficult days when you are unsure which way to turn, you must never lose sight of these overriding facts: God created you for a reason; He has important work for you to do; and He's waiting patiently for you to do it. The next step is up to you.

When God speaks to you through the Bible, prayer, circumstances, the church, or in some other way, he has a purpose in mind for your life.

Henry Blackaby and Claude King

The really committed leave the safety of the harbor, accept the risk of the open seas of faith, and set their compasses for the place of total devotion to God and whatever life adventures He plans for them.

Bill Hybels

A Prayer:

Dear Lord, let Your purposes be my purposes. Let Your priorities be my priorities. Let Your will be my will. Let Your Word be my guide. And, let me grow in faith and in wisdom today and every day. Amen

What does the Bible have to say about my life?

The Radical Answer:

Every human life (including yours) is a precious gift from God. So celebrate! And while you're at it, praise God for His blessings, and follow in the footsteps of His Son. When you do these things, you'll experience the peace and abundance that only God can give.

A Life to Be Treasured

For whoever finds me finds life and receives favor from the LORD.

Proverbs 8:35 NIV

Life can be tough sometimes, but it's also wonderful—and it's a glorious gift from God. How will you use that gift? Will you treat this day as a precious treasure from your Heavenly Father, or will you take the next 24 hours for granted? The answer should be obvious: Every day, including this one, comes gift-wrapped from God—your job is to unwrap that gift, to use it wisely, and to give thanks to the Giver.

Instead of sleepwalking through life, you and your family members must wake up and live in the precious present. Each waking moment holds the potential to celebrate, to serve, to share, or to love. Because you are a person with incalculable potential, each moment has incalculable value. Your challenge is to experience each day to the fullest as you seek to live in accordance with God's plan for your life. When you do, you'll experience His abundance and His peace.

Are you willing to treat this day (and every one hereafter) as a special gift to be savored and celebrated? You should—and if you seek to Live with a capital L, you most certainly will.

People, places, and things were never meant to give us life. God alone is the author of a fulfilling life.

Gary Smalley & John Trent

In the great orchestra we call life, you have an instrument and a song, and you owe it to God to play them both sublimely.

Max Lucado

A Prayer:

Dear Lord, You have created this glorious universe, and You have created me. Let me live my life to the fullest, and let me use my life for Your glory, today and every day. Amen

Life is an exercise in making choices. How does God want me to choose?

The Radical Answer:

God wants you to study His Word, to follow His Son, and to make choices accordingly.

Choices

I am offering you life or death, blessings or curses. Now, choose life! . . . To choose life is to love the Lord your God, obey him, and stay close to him.

Deuteronomy 30:19-20 NCV

Life is a series of decisions and choices. Each day, we make countless decisions that can bring us closer to God...or not. When we live according to God's commandments, we earn for ourselves the abundance and peace that He intends for our lives. But, when we turn our backs upon God by disobeying Him, we bring needless suffering upon ourselves and our families.

Do you seek spiritual abundance that can be yours through the person of God's only begotten Son? Then invite Christ into your heart and live according to His teachings. And, when you confront a difficult decision or a powerful temptation, seek God's wisdom and trust it.

When you do, you will receive untold blessings—not only for this day, but also for all eternity.

Life is a series of choices between the bad, the good, and the best. Everything depends on how we choose.

Vance Havner

Every day, I find countless opportunities to decide whether I will obey God and demonstrate my love for Him or try to please myself or the world system. God is waiting for my choices.

Bill Bright

We are either the masters or the victims of our attitudes. It is a matter of personal choice. Who we are today is the result of choices we made yesterday. Tomorrow, we will become what we choose today. To change means to choose to change.

John Maxwell

A Prayer:

Heavenly Father, I have many choices to make. Help me choose wisely as I follow in the footsteps of Your only begotten Son. Amen

I try to do my best, but sometimes, despite my best efforts, I make big mistakes. What does the Bible say about that?

The Radical Answer:

Time and again, the Bible preaches the power of perseverance. Setbacks, disappointments, and failures are inevitable—your response to them is optional. If you don't give up, you can turn your stumbling blocks into stepping stones . . . and you should.

Beyond Failure

Success, success to you, and success to those who help you, for your God will help you....

1 Chronicles 12:18 NIV

The occasional disappointments and failures of life are in-evitable. Such setbacks are simply the price that we must occasionally pay for our willingness to take risks as we follow our dreams. But even when we encounter bitter disappointments, we must never lose faith.

The reassuring words of Hebrews 10:36 remind us that when we persevere, we will eventually receive that which God has promised. What's required is perseverance, not perfection.

When we encounter the inevitable difficulties of life here on earth, God stands ready to protect us. Our responsibility, of course, is to ask Him for protection. When we call upon Him in heartfelt prayer, He will answer—in His own time and according to His own plan—and He will heal us. And, while we are waiting for God's plans to unfold and for His healing touch to restore us, we can be comforted in the knowledge that our Creator can overcome any obstacle, even if we cannot.

No matter how badly we have failed, we can always get up and begin again. Our God is the God of new beginnings.

Warren Wiersbe

Success or failure can be pretty well predicted by the degree to which the heart is fully in it.

John Eldredge

A Prayer:

Dear Lord, when I encounter failures and disappointments, keep me mindful that You are in control. Let me persevere—even if my soul is troubled—and let me follow Your Son, Jesus Christ, this day and forever. Amen

Sometimes it's hard to be patient. What advice can I find in God's Word?

The Radical Answer:

When you learn to be more patient with others, you'll make your world—and your heart—a better place.

The Power of Patience

Be gentle to everyone, able to teach, and patient.

2 Timothy 2:23 HCSB

We human beings are, by our very nature, impatient. We are impatient with others, impatient with ourselves, and impatient with our Creator. We want things to happen according to our own timetables, but our Heavenly Father may have other plans. That's why we must learn the art of patience.

Psalm 37:7 commands us to "rest in the Lord, and wait patiently for Him" (NKJV). But, for most of us, waiting patiently for Him is difficult. Why? Because we are fallible people who seek solutions to our problems today, if not sooner. Still, God instructs us to wait patiently for His plans to unfold, and that's exactly what we should do.

So the next time you find yourself drumming your fingers as you wait for a quick resolution to the challenges of everyday living, take a deep breath and ask God for patience. Be still before your Heavenly Father and trust His timetable: it's the peaceful way to live.

You can't step in front of God and not get in trouble. When He says, "Go three steps," don't go four.

Charles Stanley

As we wait on God, He helps us use the winds of adversity to soar above our problems. As the Bible says, "Those who wait on the LORD...shall mount up with wings like eagles."

Billy Graham

Teach us, O Lord, the disciplines of patience, for to wait is often harder than to work.

Peter Marshall

A Prayer:

Heavenly Father, let me wait quietly for You. Let me live according to Your plan and according to Your timetable. When I am hurried, slow me down. When I become impatient with others, give me empathy. Today, I want to be a patient Christian, Dear Lord, as I trust in You and in Your master plan. Amen

What does the Bible say about the example that I should set for my family?

The Radical Answer:

Your life is a sermon. The words you choose to speak may have some impact on others, but not nearly as much impact as the life you choose to live. God wants you to be a positive role model to your family, to your friends, and to the world.

What Kind of Example?

You should be an example to the believers in speech, in conduct, in love, in faith, in purity.

1 Timothy 4:12 HCSB

What kind of example are you? Are you the kind of man whose life serves as a powerful example of righteousness? Are you a man whose behavior serves as a positive role model for young people? Are you the kind of man whose actions, day in and day out, are based upon integrity, fidelity, and a love for the Lord? If so, you are not only blessed by God, but you are also a powerful force for good in a world that desperately needs positive influences such as yours.

Phillips Brooks advised, "Be such a man, and live such a life, that if every man were such as you, and every life a life like yours, this earth would be God's Paradise." And that's sound advice because our families and friends are watching . . . and so, for that matter, is God.

We urgently need people who encourage and inspire us to move toward God and away from the world's enticing pleasures.

Jim Cymbala

A holy life will produce the deepest impression. Lighthouses blow no horns; they only shine.

D. L. Moody

Our walk counts far more than our talk, always!

George Mueller

A Prayer:

Lord, make me a worthy example to my family and my friends. And, let my words and my deeds serve as a testimony to the changes You have made in my life. Let me praise You, Father, by following in the footsteps of Your Son, and let others see Him through me. Amen

I know I should be kind to other people, but sometimes it's so easy to overlook the needs of others. What does the Bible instruct me to do?

The Radical Answer:

You can't just talk about it: In order to be a kind person, you must not only think kind thoughts, you must also do kind things. So get busy! The time to be kind is now.

Kindness Is a Choice

A kind man benefits himself, but a cruel man brings disaster on himself.

Proverbs 11:17 HCSB

Christ showed His love for us by willingly sacrificing His own life so that we might have eternal life: "But God demonstrates his own love for us in this: While we were still sinners, Christ died for us" (Romans 5:8 NIV). We, as Christ's followers, are challenged to share His love with kind words on our lips and praise in our hearts.

Just as Christ has been—and will always be—the ultimate friend to His flock, so should we be Christlike in the kindness and generosity that we show toward others, especially those who are most in need.

When we walk each day with Jesus—and obey the commandments found in God's Holy Word—we become worthy ambassadors for Christ. When we share the love of Christ, we share a priceless gift with the world. As His servants, we must do no less.

Be so preoccupied with good will that you haven't room for ill will.

E. Stanley Jones

Do all the good you can. By all the means you can. In all the ways you can. In all the places you can. At all the times you can. To all the people you can. As long as ever you can.

John Wesley

A Prayer:

Help me, Lord, to see the needs of those around me. Today, let me show courtesy to those who cross my path. Today, let me spread kind words in honor of Your Son. Today, let forgiveness rule my heart. And every day, Lord, let my love for Christ be demonstrated through the acts of kindness that I offer to those who need the healing touch of the Master's hand. Amen

It's a noisy world. What does the Bible say about finding time for quiet reflection?

The Radical Answer:

Time and again, God's Word encourages believers to quiet themselves and spend silent moments with the Father. So begin each day with a few minutes of quiet time to organize your thoughts and praise your Creator.

Time for Silence

Be silent before the Lord and wait expectantly for Him.

Psalm 37:7 HCSB

Do you take time each day for an extended period of silence? And during those precious moments, do you sincerely open your heart to your Creator? If so, you are wise and you are blessed.

The world can be a noisy place, a place filled to the brim with distractions, interruptions, and frustrations. And if you're not careful, the struggles and stresses of everyday living can rob you of the peace that should rightfully be yours because of your personal relationship with Christ. So take time each day to quietly commune with your Savior. When you do, those moments of silence will enable you to participate more fully in the only source of peace that endures: God's peace.

If the pace and the push, the noise and the crowds are getting to you, it's time to stop the nonsense and find a place of solace to refresh your spirit.

Charles Swindoll

Silence is as fit a garment for devotion as any other language.

C. H. Spurgeon

There are times when to speak is to violate the moment—when silence represents the highest respect. The word for such times is reverence.

Max Lucado

Growth takes place in quietness, in hidden ways, in silence and solitude. The process is not accessible to observation.

Eugene Peterson

A Prayer:

Dear Lord, in the quiet moments of this day, I will turn my thoughts and prayers to You. In silence I will sense Your presence, and I will seek Your will for my life, knowing that when I accept Your peace, I will be blessed today and throughout eternity. Amen

Tough times are inevitable. What should I do when I encounter adversity?

The Radical Answer:

First, trust God. Next, pray early and often. Then, face your challenges head-on. And finally, remember that there's nothing you'll face today that you and God, working together, can't handle.

Tackling Tough Times

God is our refuge and strength, always ready to help in times of trouble. So we will not fear, even if earthquakes come and mountains crumble to the sea.

Psalm 46:1-2 NLT

Are you a man who has endured tough times? If so, welcome to the club! From time to time, all of us face adversity, discouragement, or disappointment. When we do, God stands ready to protect us. Psalm 147 promises, "He heals the brokenhearted, and binds their wounds" (v. 3, NIV). When we are troubled, we must call upon God, and then, in His own time and according to His own plan, He will heal us.

Life is often challenging, but as Christians, we must not be afraid. God loves us, and He will protect us. In times of hardship, He will comfort us; in times of sorrow, He will dry our tears. When we are troubled, or weak, or sorrowful, God is always with us. We must build our lives on the rock that cannot be shaken...we must trust in God. Always.

Your greatest ministry will likely come out of your greatest hurt.

Rick Warren

God will not permit any troubles to come upon us unless He has a specific plan by which great blessing can come out of the difficulty.

Peter Marshall

Jesus does not say, "There is no storm." He says, "I am here, do not toss, but trust."

Vance Havner

A Prayer:

Heavenly Father, You are my strength and my refuge. As I journey through this day, I know that I may encounter disappointments and losses. When I am troubled, let me turn to You. Keep me steady, Lord, and renew a right spirit inside of me this day and forever. Amen

What does the Bible say about the power of faith?

The Radical Answer:

Faith in God is contagious . . . and when it comes to your family's spiritual journey, no one's faith is more contagious than yours! Act, pray, praise, and trust God with the certain knowledge that your friends and family are watching . . . carefully!

When Mountains Need Moving

I assure you: If anyone says to this mountain, "Be lifted up and thrown into the sea," and does not doubt in his heart, but believes that what he says will happen, it will be done for him.

Mark 11:23 HCSB

Because we live in a demanding world, all of us have mountains to climb and mountains to move. Moving those mountains requires faith.

Are you a mountain-moving guy whose faith is evident for all to see? Or, are you a spiritual underachiever? As you think about the answer to that question, consider this: God needs more people who are willing to move mountains for His glory and for His kingdom.

Every life—including yours—is a series of wins and losses. Every step of the way, through every triumph and tragedy, God walks with you, ready and willing to strengthen you. So the next time you find your courage tested to the limit, remember to take your fears to God. If you call upon Him, you will be comforted. Whatever your challenge, whatever your trouble, God can handle it.

When you place your faith, your trust, indeed your life in the hands of your Heavenly Father, you'll be amazed at the marvelous things He can do with you and through you. So strengthen your faith through praise, through worship, through Bible study, and through prayer. And trust God's plans. With Him, all things are possible, and He stands ready to open a world of possibilities to you . . . if you have faith. And now, with no more delays, let the mountain moving begin.

Faith is confidence in the promises of God or confidence that God will do what He has promised.

Charles Stanley

A Prayer:

Dear Lord, I want faith that moves mountains. You have big plans for this world and big plans for me. Help me fulfill those plans, Father, as I follow in the footsteps of Your Son. Amen

What does the Bible say about the need to serve others?

The Radical Answer:

Whether you realize it or not, God has called you to a life of service. Your job is to find a place to serve and to get busy.

A Willingness to Serve

You address me as "Teacher" and "Master," and rightly so. That is what I am. So if I, the Master and Teacher, washed your feet, you must now wash each other's feet. I've laid down a pattern for you. What I've done, you do.

John 13:15 MSG

Jesus teaches that the most esteemed men and women are not the leaders of society or the captains of industry. To the contrary, Jesus teaches that the greatest among us are those who choose to minister and to serve.

Today, you may feel the temptation to build yourself up in the eyes of your neighbors. Resist that temptation. Instead, serve your neighbors quietly and without fanfare. Find a need and fill it . . . humbly. Lend a helping hand and share a word of kindness . . . anonymously.

Today, take the time to minister to those in need. Then, when you have done your best to serve your neighbors and to serve your God, you can rest comfortably knowing that in the eyes of God you have achieved greatness. And God's eyes, after all, are the only ones that really count.

In Jesus, the service of God and the service of the least of the brethren were one.

Dietrich Bonhoeffer

Make it a rule, and pray to God to help you to keep it, never, if possible, to lie down at night without being able to say: "I have made one human being at least a little wiser, or a little happier, or at least a little better this day."

Charles Kingsley

When you're enjoying the fulfillment and fellowship that inevitably accompanies authentic service, ministry is a joy. Instead of exhausting you, it energizes you; instead of burnout, you experience blessing.

Bill Hybels

A Prayer:

Dear Lord, when Jesus humbled Himself and became a servant, He also became an example for me. Make me a faithful steward of my gifts, and let me be a humble servant to my loved ones, to my friends, and to those in need. Amen

What does the Bible say about discipline?

The Radical Answer:

Time and again, the Bible praises discipline. A disciplined lifestyle gives you more control: The more disciplined you become, the more you can take control over your life (which, by the way, is far better than letting your life take control over you).

Discipline Now

But I discipline my body and bring it into subjection, lest, when I have preached to others, I myself should become disqualified.

1 Corinthians 9:27 NKJV

Are you a self-disciplined man? If so, congratulations . . . if not, God wants to have a little talk with you.

You live in a world in which leisure is glorified and indifference is often glamorized. But God has other plans. He did not create you to be ordinary; He created you for far greater things.

Life's greatest rewards aren't likely to fall into your lap. To the contrary, your greatest accomplishments will probably require lots of work, which is perfectly fine with God. After all, He knows that you're up to the task, and He has big plans for you. God will do His part to fulfill those plans, and the rest, of course, is up to you.

Now, are you steadfast in your determination to be a self-disciplined man? If so, congratulations . . . if not, reread this little essay—and keep reading it—until God's message finally sinks in.

If one examines the secret behind a championship football team, a magnificent orchestra, or a successful business, the principal ingredient is invariably discipline.

James Dobson

The alternative to discipline is disaster.

Vance Havner

Work is doing it. Discipline is doing it every day. Diligence is doing it well every day.

Dave Ramsey

A Prayer:
Heavenly Father, make me a man of discipline and righteousness. Let me teach others by the faithfulness of my conduct, and let me follow Your will and Your Word, today and every day. Amen

So many people around me seem to need encouragement. What should I do?

The Radical Answer:

Do you want to be successful and go far in life? Encourage others to do the same. You can't lift other people up without lifting yourself up, too. And remember the words of Oswald Chambers: "God grant that we may not hinder those who are battling their way slowly into the light."

The Gift of Encouragement

Let's see how inventive we can be in encouraging love and helping out, not avoiding worshipping together as some do but spurring each other on.

Hebrews 10:24-25 MSG

Life is a team sport, and all of us need occasional pats on the back from our teammates. This world can be a difficult place, a place where many of our friends and family members are troubled by the challenges of everyday life. And since we cannot always be certain who needs our help, we should strive to speak helpful words to all those who cross our paths.

In the book of Ephesians, Paul writes, "Do not let any unwholesome talk come out of your mouths, but only what is helpful for building others up according to their needs, that it may benefit those who listen" (4:29 NIV). Paul reminds us that when we choose our words carefully, we can have a powerful impact on those around us.

Today, let us be cheerful Christians; let us keep smiles on our faces and encouraging words on our lips. By blessing others, we also bless ourselves, and, at the same time, we honor to the One who gave His life for us.

We urgently need people who encourage and inspire us to move toward God and away from the world's enticing pleasures.

Jim Cymbala

A lot of people have gone further than they thought they could because someone else thought they could.

Zig Ziglar

A Prayer:

Dear Lord, make me a man who is quick to celebrate the accomplishments of others. Make me a source of genuine, lasting encouragement to my family and friends. And let my words and deeds be worthy of Your Son, the One who gives me strength and salvation, this day and for all eternity. Amen

Our family has so much to be thankful for. What should we do?

The Radical Answer:

Don't overlook God's gifts: Every sunrise represents yet another beautifully wrapped gift from God. Unwrap it; treasure it; use it; and give thanks to the Giver.

Saying "Thanks" to God

Give thanks in all circumstances; for this is God's will for you in Christ Jesus.

1 Thessalonians 5:18 NIV

The words of 1 Thessalonians 5:18 remind us to give thanks in every circumstance of life. But sometimes, when our hearts are troubled and our spirits are crushed, we don't feel like celebrating. Yet even when the clouds of despair darken our lives, God offers us His love, His strength, and His grace. And as believers, we must thank Him.

Have you thanked God today for blessings that are too numerous to count? Have you offered Him your heartfelt prayers and your wholehearted praise? If not, it's time to slow down and to offer a prayer of thanksgiving to the One who has given you life on earth and life eternal.

No matter our circumstances, we owe God so much more than we can ever repay, and the least we can do is to thank Him.

We ought to give thanks for all fortune: if it is good, because it is good, if bad, because it works in us patience, humility, and the contempt of this world along with the hope of our eternal country.

C. S. Lewis

The words "thank" and "think" come from the same root word. If we would think more, we would thank more.

Warren Wiersbe

It is only with gratitude that life becomes rich.

Dietrich Bonhoeffer

A Prayer:

Lord, You have blessed me with a loving family—make me a man who is thankful, loving, responsible, and wise. I praise You, Father, for the gift of Your Son and for the gift of salvation. Let me be a joyful Christian and a worthy example, this day and every day that I live. Amen

What does God's Word say about work?

The Radical Answer:

Work is honored by God—He expects each of us to do our fair share. So encourage your friends and family to find meaningful work that they enjoy. People who are passionate about their professions are usually more successful than people who aren't.

Getting the Work Done

Do not be lazy but work hard, serving the Lord with all your heart.

Romans 12:11 NCV

Providing for your family requires work and lots of it. And as a hardworking man, you have earned the gratitude of your loved ones and the praise of your Heavenly Father.

It has been said that there are no shortcuts to any place worth going. Making the grade in today's competitive workplace is not easy. In fact, it can be very difficult indeed. But, even when the workday is long and the workload is difficult, we must not become discouraged.

God did not create us for lives of mediocrity; He created us for far greater things. Earning great things usually requires determination, persistence, and hard work—which is perfectly fine with God. After all, He knows that we're up to the task, and He has big plans for us. Very big plans.

Chiefly the mold of a man's fortune is in his own hands.

Francis Bacon

People who work for money only are usually miserable, because there is no fulfillment and no meaning to what they do.

Dave Ramsey

If you want to reach your potential, you need to add a strong work ethic to your talent.

John Maxwell

It may be that the day of judgment will dawn tomorrow; in that case, we shall gladly stop working for a better tomorrow. But not before.

Dietrich Bonhoeffer

A Prayer:

Lord, let me be an industrious worker in Your fields. Those fields are ripe, Lord, and Your workers are few. Let me be counted as Your faithful, diligent servant today, and every day. Amen

Some things are very hard to accept. What should I do?

The Radical Answer:

You must learn to accept the things you cannot change—since you can't change the past, you must learn to accept it. Otherwise, you'll make yourself miserable as you continually rehash yesterday's disappointments.

Accepting Life

The Lord says, "Forget what happened before, and do not think about the past. Look at the new thing I am going to do. It is already happening. Don't you see it? I will make a road in the desert and rivers in the dry land."

Isaiah 43:18-19 NCV

Sometimes, we must accept life on its terms, not our own. Life has a way of unfolding, not as we will, but as it will. And sometimes, there is precious little we can do to change things.

When events transpire that are beyond our control, we have a choice: we can either learn the art of acceptance, or we can make ourselves miserable as we struggle to change the unchangeable.

We must entrust the things we cannot change to God. Once we have done so, we can prayerfully and faithfully tackle the important work that He has placed before us: doing something about the things we can change . . . and doing it sooner rather than later.

The one true way of dying to self is the way of patience, meekness, humility, and resignation to God.

Andrew Murray

Prayer may not get us what we want, but it will teach us to want what we need.

Vance Havner

Trust the past to God's mercy, the present to God's love, and the future to God's providence.

St. Augustine

A Prayer:

Dear Lord, let me live in the present, not the past. Let me focus on my blessings, not my sorrows. Give me the wisdom to be thankful for the gifts that I do have, and not bitter about the things that I don't have. Let me accept what was, let me give thanks for what is, and let me have faith in what most surely will be: the promise of eternal life with You. Amen

Sometimes life is difficult. When I'm fearful for myself or my family, what should I do?

The Radical Answer:

Ask God for strength and wisdom. And above all, trust the Lord to solve problems that are simply too big for you to solve. When you turn everything over to God, you can live courageously.

Courage for Difficult Days

Be strong and courageous, and do the work. Do not be afraid or discouraged, for the Lord God, my God, is with you.

1 Chronicles 28:20 NIV

Being a godly man in this difficult world is no easy task. Ours is a time of uncertainty and danger, a time when even the most courageous men have legitimate cause for concern. But as believers we can live courageously, knowing that we have been saved by a loving Father and His only begotten Son.

Are you anxious? Take those anxieties to God. Are you troubled? Take your troubles to Him. Does the world seem to be trembling beneath your feet? Seek protection from the One who cannot be moved. The same God who created the universe will protect you if you ask Him...so ask Him. And then live courageously, knowing that even in these troubled times, God is always as near as your next breath.

Take courage. We walk in the wilderness today and in the Promised Land tomorrow.

D. L. Moody

Do not let Satan deceive you into being afraid of God's plans for your life.

R. A. Torrey

The fear of God is the death of every other fear.

C. H. Spurgeon

Our Lord is searching for people who will make a difference. Christians dare not dissolve into the background or blend into the neutral scenery of the world.

Charles Swindoll

A Prayer:

Lord, at times, this world is a fearful place. Yet, You have promised me that You are with me always. With You as my protector, I am not afraid. Today, Dear Lord, let me live courageously as I place my trust in You. Amen

Is the Bible really God's Word, or is it simply another book?

The Radical Answer:

The Bible is the best-selling book of all time . . . for good reason. Ruth Bell Graham, wife of evangelist Billy Graham, believes in the importance of God's Word: "The Reference Point for the Christian is the Bible. All values, judgments, and attitudes must be gauged in relationship to this Reference Point." Make certain that you're an avid reader of God's best-seller, and make sure that you keep reading it as long as you live!

Nourished by the Word

You will be a good servant of Christ Jesus, constantly nourished on the words of the faith and of the sound doctrine which you have been following.

1 Timothy 4:6 NASB

God's Word is unlike any other book. The Bible is a roadmap for life here on earth and for life eternal. As Christians, we are called upon to study God's Holy Word, to trust its promises, to follow its commandments, and to share its Good News with the world.

As believers, we must study the Bible and meditate upon its meaning for our lives. Otherwise, we deprive ourselves of a priceless gift from our Creator. God's Holy Word is, indeed, a transforming, life-changing, one-of-a-kind treasure. And, a passing acquaintance with the Good Book is insufficient for Christians who seek to obey God's Word and to understand His will. After all, neither man nor woman should live by bread alone.

Try to get saturated with the gospel.

C. H. Spurgeon

God gives us a compass and a Book of promises and principles—the Bible—and lets us make our decisions day by day as we sense the leading of His Spirit. This is how we grow.

Warren Wiersbe

It takes calm, thoughtful, prayerful meditation on the Word to extract its deepest nourishment.

Vance Havner

A Prayer:

Heavenly Father, Your Word is a light unto the world; I will study it and trust it, and share it. In all that I do, help me be a worthy witness for You as I share the Good News of Your perfect Son and Your perfect Word. Amen

What does God's Word say about grace?

The Radical Answer:

God's grace is always available. Jim Cymbala writes, "No one is beyond his grace. No situation, anywhere on earth, it too hard for God." If you sincerely seek God's grace, He will give it freely. So ask, and you will receive.

The Ultimate Treasure: God's Grace

Grace to you and peace from God our Father and the Lord Jesus Christ.

Philippians 1:2 NASB

Someone has said that GRACE stands for God's Redemption At Christ's Expense. It's true—God sent His Son so that we might be redeemed from our sins. In doing so, our Heavenly Father demonstrated His infinite mercy and His infinite love. We have received countless gifts from God, but none can compare with the gift of salvation. God's grace is the ultimate gift, and we owe Him the ultimate in thanksgiving.

The gift of eternal life is the priceless possession of everyone who accepts God's Son as Lord and Savior. We return our Savior's love by welcoming Him into our hearts and sharing His message and His love. When we do so, we are blessed today and forever.

The grace of God is sufficient for all our needs, for every problem, and for every difficulty, for every broken heart, and for every human sorrow.

Peter Marshall

You don't earn grace, and you don't deserve grace; you simply receive it as God's loving gift, and then share it with others.

Warren Wiersbe

Grace is an outrageous blessing bestowed freely on a totally undeserving recipient.

Bill Hybels

A Prayer:

Lord, You have saved me by Your grace. Keep me mindful that Your grace is a gift that I can accept but cannot earn. I praise You for that priceless gift, today and forever. Let me share the good news of Your grace with a world that desperately needs Your healing touch. Amen

We live in a materialistic world. What does the Bible have to say about that?

The Radical Answer:
Too much stuff doesn't ensure happiness. In fact, having too much stuff can actually prevent happiness.

Beyond Materialism

Don't collect for yourselves treasures on earth, where moth and rust destroy and where thieves break in and steal. But collect for yourselves treasures in heaven, where neither moth nor rust destroys, and where thieves don't break in and steal. For where your treasure is, there your heart will be also.

Matthew 6:19-21 HCSB

In our modern society, we need money to live. But as Christians, we must never make the acquisition of money the central focus of our lives. Money is a tool, but it should never overwhelm our sensibilities. The focus of life must be squarely on things spiritual, not things material.

Whenever we place our love for material possessions above our love for God—or when we yield to the countless other temptations of everyday living—we find ourselves engaged in a struggle between good and evil, a clash between God and Satan. Our responses to these struggles have implications that echo throughout our families and throughout our communities. Let us choose wisely by freeing ourselves from that subtle yet powerful temptation: the temptation to love the world more than we love God.

When possessions become our god, we become materialistic and greedy . . . and we forfeit our contentment and our joy.

Charles Swindoll

He is no fool who gives what he cannot keep to gain what he cannot lose.

Jim Elliot

If you want to be truly happy, you won't find it on an endless quest for more stuff. You'll find it in receiving God's generosity and in passing that generosity along.

Bill Hybels

A Prayer:

Lord, my greatest possession is my relationship with You through Jesus Christ. You have promised that, when I first seek Your kingdom and Your righteousness, You will give me whatever I need. Let me trust You completely, Lord, for my needs, both material and spiritual, this day and always. Amen

What does the Bible say about following in Jesus' footsteps?

The Radical Answer:

If you want to follow in Christ's footsteps . . . welcome Him into your heart, obey His commandments, and share His never-ending love.

Follow Him

"Follow Me," Jesus told them, "and I will make you into fishers of men!" Immediately they left their nets and followed Him.

Mark 1:17-18 HCSB

Whom will you walk with today? Will you walk with people who worship the ways of the world? Or will you walk with the Son of God?

Jesus walks with you. Are you walking with Him? Hopefully, you will choose to walk with Him today and every day of your life.

Jesus has called upon believers of every generation (and that includes you) to follow in His footsteps. And God's Word promises that when you follow in Christ's footsteps, you will learn how to live freely and lightly (Matthew 11:28-30).

Are you worried about the day ahead? Be confident in God's power. He will never desert you. Are you concerned about the future? Be courageous and call upon God. He will protect you. Are you confused? Listen to the quiet voice of your Heavenly Father. He is not a God of confusion. Talk with God; listen to Him; follow His commandments . . . and walk with His Son—starting now.

Imagine the spiritual strength the disciples drew from walking hundreds of miles with Jesus…(3 John 4).

John Maxwell

Our responsibility is to feed from Him, to stay close to Him, to follow Him—because sheep easily go astray—so that we eternally experience the protection and companionship of our Great Shepherd the Lord Jesus Christ.

Franklin Graham

We have in Jesus Christ a perfect example of how to put God's truth into practice.

Bill Bright

A Prayer:
Dear Lord, You sent Jesus to save the world and to save me. I thank You for Jesus, and I will do my best to follow Him, today and forever. Amen

Sometimes my life doesn't seem very exciting. Why should I be excited about life?

The Radical Answer:

Today is a cause for celebration: Psalm 118:24 has clear instructions for the coming day: "This is the day which the LORD has made; let us rejoice and be glad in it." Plan your day—and your life—accordingly.

Celebrate!

Celebrate God all day, every day. I mean, revel in him!

Philippians 4:4 MSG

Are you a man who celebrates life? Hopefully you are! God has richly blessed you, and He wants you to rejoice in His gifts.

God fills each day to the brim with possibilities, and He challenges each of us to use our gifts for the glory of His kingdom. When we honor the Father and place Him at the center of our lives, every day becomes a cause for celebration.

Today is a non-renewable resource—once it's gone, it's gone forever. Our responsibility—as believers—is to use this day in the service of God's will and in the service of

His people. When we do so, we enrich our own lives and the lives of those whom we love. And the Father smiles.

Let God have you, and let God love you—and don't be surprised if your heart begins to hear music you've never heard and your feet learn to dance as never before.

Max Lucado

Some of us seem so anxious about avoiding hell that we forget to celebrate our journey toward heaven.

Philip Yancey

If you can forgive the person you were, accept the person you are, and believe in the person you will become, you are headed for joy. So celebrate your life.

Barbara Johnson

A Prayer:

Dear Lord, You have given me many reasons to celebrate. Today, let me choose an attitude of cheerfulness. Let me be a joyful Christian, Lord, quick to laugh and slow to anger. Let me praise You, Lord, and give thanks for Your blessings. Today is Your creation; let me celebrate it...and You. Amen

What does the Bible say about optimism?

The Radical Answer:

The Bible promises that if you've give your heart to Jesus, your eternal future is secure. So even when times are tough, you can be hopeful, joyful, and optimistic.

Optimism Now

I can do everything through him that gives me strength.

Philippians 4:13 NIV

The words of Psalm 118:24 remind us of a profound yet simple truth: "This is the day which the LORD hath made; we will rejoice and be glad in it" (KJV).

As each day unfolds, we are literally surrounded by more opportunities than we can count—opportunities to improve our own lives and the lives of those we love. God's Word promises that each of us possess the ability to experience earthly peace and spiritual abundance.

So, as we face the inevitable challenges of life here on earth, we must not become discouraged. We must, instead, arm ourselves with the promises of God and when we do, we can expect the very best that life—and God—has to offer.

The popular idea of faith is of a certain obstinate optimism: the hope, tenaciously held in the face of trouble, that the universe is fundamentally friendly and things may get better.

J. I. Packer

It is a remarkable thing that some of the most optimistic and enthusiastic people you will meet are those who have been through intense suffering.

Warren Wiersbe

Christ can put a spring in your step and a thrill in your heart. Optimism and cheerfulness are products of knowing Christ.

Billy Graham

A Prayer:

Lord, You care for me, You love me, and You have given me the priceless gift of eternal life through Your Son Jesus. Because of You, Lord, I have every reason to live each day with celebration and hope. Help me to face this day with a spirit of optimism and thanksgiving so that I may lift the spirits of those I meet as I share the Good News of Your Son. And, let me focus my thoughts on You and Your incomparable gifts today and forever. Amen

When I'm overcome by worries, what should I do . . . and where should I turn?

The Radical Answer:

Categorize your worries. Carefully divide your areas of concern into two categories: those things you can control and those you cannot control. Once you've done so, spend your time working to resolve the things you can control, and entrust everything else to God.

Beyond Worry

Jesus said, "Don't let your hearts be troubled. Trust in God, and trust in me."

John 14:1 NCV

In the game of life, you win some, and you lose some. Life is risky business; you live in an uncertain world, a world in which trouble may come calling at any moment. No wonder you may find yourself feeling a little panicky at times.

Do you sometimes spend more time worrying about a problem than you spend solving it? If so, here's a strategy for dealing with your worries: Take them to God. Take your troubles to Him; take your fears to Him; take your doubts to Him; take your weaknesses to Him; take your sorrows to Him . . . and leave them all there. Period.

God is the Rock that cannot be moved. When you build your life upon that Rock, you have absolutely no need to worry . . . not now, not ever.

The beginning of anxiety is the end of faith, and the beginning of true faith is the end of anxiety.

George Mueller

God is bigger than your problems. Whatever worries press upon you today, put them in God's hands and leave them there.

Billy Graham

Today is the tomorrow we worried about yesterday.

Dennis Swanberg

A Prayer:

Dear Lord, wherever I find myself, let me celebrate more and worry less. When my faith begins to waver, help me to trust You more. Then, with praise on my lips and the love of Your Son in my heart, let me live courageously, faithfully, prayerfully, and thankfully this day and every day. Amen

I have big dreams. What should I do about them?

The Radical Answer:

Making your dreams come true requires work. John Maxwell writes, "The gap between your vision and your present reality can only be filled through a commitment to maximize your potential." Enough said.

Big Dreams

Live full lives, full in the fullness of God. God can do anything, you know—far more than you could ever imagine or guess or request in your wildest dreams! He does it not by pushing us around but by working within us, his Spirit deeply and gently within us.

Ephesians 3:19-20 MSG

Are you willing to entertain the possibility that God has big plans in store for you and your family? Hopefully so. Yet sometimes, especially if you've recently experienced a life-altering disappointment, you may find it difficult to envision a brighter future for yourself and your family. If so, it's time to reconsider your own capabilities . . . and God's.

Your Heavenly Father created you with unique gifts and untapped talents; your job is to tap them. When you do, you'll begin to feel an increasing sense of confidence in yourself and in your future.

It takes courage to dream big dreams. You will discover that courage when you do three things: accept the past, trust God to handle the future, and make the most of the time He has given you today.

Nothing is too difficult for God, and no dreams are too big for Him—not even yours. So start living—and dreaming—accordingly.

You cannot out-dream God.

John Eldredge

Allow your dreams a place in your prayers and plans. God-given dreams can help you move into the future He is preparing for you.

Barbara Johnson

A Prayer:

Dear Lord, give me the courage to dream and the faithfulness to trust in Your perfect plan. When I am worried or weary, give me strength for today and hope for tomorrow. Keep me mindful of Your healing power, Your infinite love, and Your eternal salvation. Amen

What does the Bible have to say about the importance of being a joyful person?

The Radical Answer:

God's Word instructs us to be joyful. And we must remember that joy does not depend upon our circumstances, but upon our relationship with God.

Real Joy

I've told you these things for a purpose: that my joy might be your joy, and your joy wholly mature.

John 15:11 MSG

Are you a man whose joy is evident for all to see? If so, congratulations: you're doing God's will. Psalm 100 reminds us that, as believers, we have every reason to celebrate: "Shout for joy to the LORD, all the earth. Worship the LORD with gladness" (vv. 1-2 NIV). Yet sometimes, amid the inevitable hustle and bustle of life here on earth, we can forfeit—albeit temporarily—the joy that God intends for our lives.

If you find yourself feeling discouraged or worse, it's time to slow down and have a quiet conversation with your Creator. If your heart is heavy, open the door of your soul to the Father and to His only begotten Son. Christ offers you His peace and His joy. Accept it and share it freely, just as Christ has freely shared His joy with you.

Joy comes from knowing God loves me and knows who I am and where I'm going . . . that my future is secure as I rest in Him.

James Dobson

When I met Christ, I felt that I had swallowed sunshine.

E. Stanley Jones

I choose joy. I will refuse the temptation to be cynical; cynicism is the tool of a lazy thinker. I will refuse to see people as anything less than human beings, created by God. I will refuse to see any problem as anything less than an opportunity to see God.

Max Lucado

A Prayer:

Dear Lord, You have blessed me with a loving family; make me thankful, loving, responsible, and wise. I praise You, Father, for the gift of Your Son and for the gift of salvation. Let me be a joyful Christian and a worthy example, this day and every day that I live. Amen

How best can I teach my family and friends about the importance of self-discipline?

The Radical Answer:

If you want to teach discipline, you must be disciplined in your own approach to life. You can't teach it if you won't live it.

The Rewards of Discipline

Discipline yourself for the purpose of godliness.

1 Timothy 4:7 NASB

Wise men teach the importance of discipline using both words and examples. Disciplined men understand that God doesn't reward laziness or misbehavior. To the contrary, God expects His believers to lead lives that are above reproach. And, He punishes those who disobey His commandments.

In Proverbs 28:19, God's message is clear: "He who works his land will have abundant food, but the one who chases fantasies will have his fill of poverty" (NIV). When we work diligently and consistently, we can expect a bountiful harvest. But we must never expect the harvest to precede the labor. First, we must lead lives of discipline and obedience; then, we will reap the never-ending rewards that God has promised.

Work is doing it. Discipline is doing it every day. Diligence is doing it well every day.

Dave Ramsey

As we seek to become disciples of Jesus Christ, we should never forget that the word disciple is directly related to the word discipline. To be a disciple of the Lord Jesus Christ is to know his discipline.

Dennis Swanberg

Discipline is training that develops and corrects.

Charles Stanley

The alternative to discipline is disaster.

Vance Havner

A Prayer:

Lord, let me be Your faithful servant, Lord, and let me serve as an example of faithfulness by my conduct and by my communications. Let me follow Your commandments just as surely as I teach other people to obey You and to love You. Amen

Sometimes it's hard for me to forgive the people who have hurt me. What does the Bible say about that?

The Radical Answer:

God's Word instructs you to forgive others . . . no exceptions. Forgiveness is its own reward and bitterness is its own punishment. So guard your words and your thoughts accordingly.

Forgiveness Now

Then Peter came to him and asked, "Lord, how often should I forgive someone who sins against me? Seven times?" "No!" Jesus replied, "seventy times seven!"

Matthew 18:21-22 NLT

Even the most mild-mannered men will, on occasion, have reason to become angry with the shortcomings of family members and friends. But wise men are quick to forgive others, just as God has forgiven them.

Forgiveness is God's commandment, but oh, how difficult a commandment it can be to follow. Being frail, fallible, imperfect human beings, we are quick to anger, quick to blame, slow to forgive, and even slower to forget. No matter. Forgiveness, no matter how difficult, is God's way, and it must be our way, too.

If, in your heart, you hold bitterness against even a single person, forgive. If there exists even one person, alive or dead, whom you have not forgiven, follow God's commandment and His will for your life: forgive. If you are embittered against yourself for some past mistake or shortcoming, forgive. Then, to the best of your abilities, forget. And move on. Hatred and bitterness and regret are not part of God's plan for your life. Forgiveness is.

There is always room for more loving forgiveness within our homes.

James Dobson

Learning how to forgive and forget is one of the secrets of a happy Christian life.

Warren Wiersbe

A Prayer:

Lord, I know that I need to forgive others just as You have forgiven me. Help me to be an example of forgiveness to my family and friends. Keep me mindful, Father, that I am never fully liberated until I have been freed from the chains of bitterness—and that You offer me that freedom through Your Son, Christ Jesus. Amen

What does the Bible say about enthusiasm?

The Radical Answer:

Be enthusiastic about your faith: John Wesley wrote, "You don't have to advertise a fire. Get on fire for God and the world will come to watch you burn." When you allow yourself to become extremely enthusiastic about your faith, other people will notice—and so will God.

Enthused About Life

Whatever you do, do it enthusiastically, as something done for the Lord and not for men.

Colossians 3:23 HCSB

Do you see each day as a glorious opportunity to serve God and to do His will? Are you enthused about life, or do you struggle through each day giving scarcely a thought to God's blessings? Are you constantly praising God for His gifts, and are you sharing His Good News with the world? And are you excited about the possibilities for service that God has placed before you, whether at home, at work, or at church? You should be.

You are the recipient of Christ's sacrificial love. Accept it enthusiastically and share it fervently. Jesus deserves your enthusiasm; the world deserves it; and you deserve the experience of sharing it.

When we wholeheartedly commit ourselves to God, there is nothing mediocre or run-of-the-mill about us. To live for Christ is to be passionate about our Lord and about our lives.

Jim Gallery

Wherever you are, be all there. Live to the hilt every situation you believe to be the will of God.

Jim Elliot

Catch on fire with enthusiasm and people will come for miles to watch you burn.

John Wesley

We act as though comfort and luxury were the chief requirements of life, when all we need to make us really happy is something to be enthusiastic about.

Charles Kingsley

A Prayer:

Dear Lord, You have called me not to a life of mediocrity, but to a life of passion. Today, I will be an enthusiastic follower of Your Son, and I will share His Good News—and His love—with all who cross my path. Amen

What does the Bible teach us about leadership, and about leading my family?

The Radical Answer:

Since leadership comes in many forms, you can lead your family in your own way using your own style. Leadership is a responsibility that must not be taken lightly. If you choose to lead, you should first choose to follow Jesus.

The Need to Lead

Good leadership is a channel of water controlled by God; he directs it to whatever ends he chooses.

Proverbs 21:1 MSG

As the leader of your family, you have a profound responsibility to your loved ones and to your God. If you desire to be an obedient servant to your Heavenly Father, you must lead your family according to His Holy Word. To do otherwise is to rob your loved ones of the peace and abundance that is rightfully theirs through the person of Jesus Christ.

Our world needs Christian leaders, and so does your family. So make this pledge and keep it: vow to become the godly leader that God intends you to be. Your family needs you, and you need the experience of leading them in the service of your Lord.

The test of a leader is taking the vision from me to we.

John Maxwell

What do we Christians chiefly value in our leaders? The answer seems to be not their holiness, but their gifts and skills and resources. The thought that only holy people are likely to be spiritually useful does not loom large in our minds.

J. I. Packer

Leaders must learn how to wait. Often their followers don't always see as far as they see or have the faith that they have.

Warren Wiersbe

People who inspire others are those who see invisible bridges at the end of dead-end streets.

Charles Swindoll

A Prayer:

Dear Lord, when I find myself in a position of leadership, let me seek Your will and obey Your commandments. Make me a person of integrity and wisdom, Lord, and make me a worthy example to my family. Let me be a Christ-centered leader, and let me turn to You, Father, for guidance, for courage, for wisdom, and for love. Amen

God has given me special talents and unique opportunities. What should I so with my talents?

The Radical Answer:

You, like every other person on earth, possess special abilities that can be nurtured carefully or ignored totally. The challenge, of course, is to do the former and to avoid the latter.

Using Your Gifts

I remind you to keep ablaze the gift of God that is in you.

2 Timothy 1:6 HCSB

God gives each of us a unique assortment of talents and opportunities. And our Heavenly Father instructs us to be faithful stewards of the gifts that He bestows upon us. But we live in a world that encourages us to do otherwise.

Ours is a society that is filled to the brim with countless opportunities to squander our time, our resources, and our talents. So we must be watchful for distractions and temptations that might lead us astray.

God has blessed you with unique opportunities to serve Him, and He has given you every tool that you need to do so. Today, accept this challenge: value the talent that God has given you, nourish it, make it grow, and share it with the world. After all, the best way to say "Thank You" for God's gifts is to use them.

God often reveals His direction for our lives through the way He made us . . . with a certain personality and unique skills.

Bill Hybels

You are the only person on earth who can use your ability.

Zig Ziglar

Employ whatever God has entrusted you with, in doing good, all possible good, in every possible kind and degree.

John Wesley

A Prayer:

Father, You have given me abilities to be used for the glory of Your kingdom. Give me the courage and the perseverance to use those talents. Keep me mindful that all my gifts come from You, Lord. Let me be Your faithful, humble servant, and let me give You all the glory and all the praise. Amen

Sometimes I have trouble focusing my thoughts and energies. What does the Bible say about that?

The Radical Answer:

The Lord wants you to focus your thoughts, your energies, your emotions, and your prayers on the things that really matter, and that means putting God first and family next.

Too Many Distractions?

Look straight ahead, and fix your eyes on what lies before you. Mark out a straight path for your feet; then stick to the path and stay safe. Don't get sidetracked; keep your feet from following evil.

Proverbs 4:25-27 NLT

All of us must live through those days when the traffic jams, the computer crashes, and the dog makes a main course out of our homework. But, when we find ourselves distracted by the minor frustrations of life, we must catch ourselves, take a deep breath, and lift our thoughts upward.

Although we may, at times, struggle mightily to rise above the distractions of everyday living, we need never struggle alone. God is here—eternal and faithful, with infinite patience and love—and, if we reach out to Him, He will restore our sense of perspective, He will give peace to our souls, and He will help us focus on the things that really matter.

As long as Jesus is one of many options, he is no option.

Max Lucado

Only the man who follows the command of Jesus single-mindedly and unresistingly let his yoke rest upon him, finds his burden easy, and under its gentle pressure receives the power to persevere in the right way.

Dietrich Bonhoeffer

Paul did one thing. Most of us dabble in forty things. Are you a doer or a dabbler?

Vance Havner

Give me the person who says, "This one thing I do, and not these fifty things I dabble in."

D. L. Moody

A Prayer:

Dear Lord, help me to face this day with a spirit of optimism and thanksgiving. And let me focus my thoughts on You and Your incomparable gifts. Amen

What does the Bible say about following my conscience?

The Radical Answer:

That quiet little voice inside your head will guide you down the right path if you listen carefully. Very often, your conscience will actually tell you what God wants you to do. So listen, learn, and behave accordingly.

You and Your Conscience

If the way you live isn't consistent with what you believe, then it's wrong.

Romans 14:23 MSG

Billy Graham correctly observed, "Most of us follow our conscience as we follow a wheelbarrow. We push it in front of us in the direction we want to go." To do so, of course, is a profound mistake. Yet all of us, on occasion, have failed to listen to the voice that God planted in our hearts, and all of us have suffered the consequences.

God gave you a conscience for a very good reason: to make your path conform to His will. Wise believers make it a practice to listen carefully to that quiet internal voice. Count yourself among that number. When your conscience speaks, listen and learn. In all likelihood, God is trying to get His message through. And in all likelihood, it is a message that you desperately need to hear.

To go against one's conscience is neither safe nor right. Here I stand. I cannot do otherwise.

Martin Luther

The convicting work of the Holy Spirit awakens, disturbs, and judges.

Franklin Graham

The beginning of backsliding means your conscience does not answer to the truth.

Oswald Sanders

A good conscience is a continual feast.

Francis Bacon

A Prayer:

Dear Lord, You speak to me through the gift of Your Holy Word. And, Father, You speak to me through that still small voice that tells me right from wrong. Let me follow Your way, Lord, and, in these quiet moments, show me Your plan for this day, that I might serve You. Amen

Sometimes I'm tempted to give up. What advice does the Bible have for me?

The Radical Answer:

The world encourages instant gratification but God's work takes time. So remember the words of C. H. Spurgeon: "By perseverance, the snail reached the ark."

The Power of Perseverance

For you need endurance, so that after you have done God's will, you may receive what was promised.

Hebrews 10:36 HCSB

The occasional disappointments and failures of life are inevitable. Such setbacks are simply the price that we must pay for our willingness to take risks as we follow our dreams. But even when we encounter setbacks, we must never lose faith.

The reassuring words of Hebrews 10:36 serve as a comforting reminder that perseverance indeed pays: "You have need of endurance, so that when you have done the will of God, you may receive what was promised" (NASB).

Are you willing to trust God's Word? And are you willing to keep "fighting the good fight," even when you've experienced unexpected difficulties? If so, you may soon be surprised at the creative ways that God finds to help determined people like you . . . people who possess the wisdom and the courage to persevere.

Jesus taught that perseverance is the essential element in prayer.

E. M. Bounds

Battles are won in the trenches, in the grit and grime of courageous determination; they are won day by day in the arena of life.

Charles Swindoll

In the Bible, patience is not a passive acceptance of circumstances. It is a courageous perseverance in the face of suffering and difficulty.

Warren Wiersbe

A Prayer:

Lord, when life is difficult, I am tempted to abandon hope in the future. But You are my God, and I can draw strength from You. Let me trust You, Father, in good times and in bad times. Let me persevere—even if my soul is troubled—and let me follow Your Son Jesus Christ this day and forever. Amen

Sometimes, it's easy for me to become angry. What does the Bible say about anger?

The Radical Answer:

The Bible warns us time and again that anger is only one letter away from danger. So the next time you're tempted to lose your cool, walk away before you get carried away.

Beyond Anger

But now you must also put away all the following: anger, wrath, malice, slander, and filthy language from your mouth.

Colossians 3:8 HCSB

The frustrations of everyday living can sometimes get the better of us, and we allow minor disappointments to cause us major problems. When we allow ourselves to become overly irritated by the inevitable ups and downs of life, and we become overstressed, overheated, over-anxious, and just plain angry.

When you allow yourself to become angry, you are certain to defeat at least one person: yourself. When you allow the minor frustrations of everyday life to hijack your emotions, you do harm to yourself and to your loved ones. So today and every day, guard yourself against the kind of angry thinking that inevitably takes a toll on your emotions and your relationships.

As the old saying goes, "Anger usually improves nothing but the arch of a cat's back." So don't allow feelings of anger or frustration to rule your life, or, for that matter, your day—your life is simply too short for that, and you deserve much better treatment than that . . . from yourself.

Anger is the noise of the soul; the unseen irritant of the heart; the relentless invader of silence.

Max Lucado

Is there somebody who's always getting your goat? Talk to the Shepherd.

Anonymous

When you strike out in anger, you may miss the other person, but you will always hit yourself.

Jim Gallery

A Prayer:

Lord, sometimes, it is so easy to lose my temper and my perspective. When anger burdens my soul, enable me to calm myself and to be a witness to Your truth and righteousness. Let other people see me as a model of kindness and forgiveness, today and every day. Amen

What does the Bible say about prayer?

The Radical Answer:

Pray early and often: One way to make sure that your heart is in tune with God is to pray often. The more you talk to the Father, the more He will talk to you.

Too Busy to Pray?

If my people who are called by my name, will humble themselves and pray and seek my face and turn from their wicked ways, then will I hear from heaven and will forgive their sin and will heal their land.

2 Chronicles 7:14 NIV

Does your family pray together often, or just at church? Are you a little band of prayer warriors, or have you retreated from God's battlefield? Do you and yours pray only at mealtimes, or do you pray much more often than that? The answer to these questions will determine, to a surprising extent, the level of your family's spiritual health.

Jesus made it clear to His disciples: they should pray always. And so should you. Genuine, heartfelt prayer changes things and it changes you. When you lift your heart to the Father, you open yourself to a never-ending source of divine wisdom and infinite love.

Your family's prayers are powerful. So, as you go about your daily activities, remember God's instructions: "Rejoice always! Pray constantly. Give thanks in everything, for this is God's will for you in Christ Jesus" (1 Thessalonians 5:16-18 HCSB). Start praying in the morning and keep praying until you fall off to sleep at night. And rest assured: God is always listening, and He always wants to hear from you and your family.

Prayer connects us with God's limitless potential.

Henry Blackaby

God shapes the world by prayer. The more praying there is in the world, the better the world will be, and the mightier will be the forces against evil.

E. M. Bounds

A Prayer:

Dear Lord, I will open my heart to You. I will take my concerns, my fears, my plans, and my hopes to You in prayer. And, then, I will trust the answers that You give. You are my loving Father, and I will accept Your will for my life today and every day that I live. Amen

I have challenges that seem overwhelming at times. What should I do?

The Radical Answer:

Remember that whatever the size of your challenge, God is bigger. Trust Him to solve the problems that are simply too big for you tackle.

God Can Handle It

Cast your burden on the Lord, and He will support you; He will never allow the righteous to be shaken.

Psalm 55:22 HCSB

It's a promise that is made over and over again in the Bible: Whatever "it" is, God can handle it.

Life isn't always easy. Far from it! Sometimes, life can be very, very difficult, indeed. But even when the storm clouds form overhead, even during our darkest moments, we're protected by a loving Heavenly Father.

When we're worried, God can reassure us; when we're sad, God can comfort us. When our hearts are broken, God is not just near; He is here. So we must lift our thoughts and prayers to Him. When we do, He will answer our prayers. Why? Because He is our Shepherd, and He has promised to protect us now and forever.

The next time you're disappointed, don't panic. Don't give up. Just be patient and let God remind you he's still in control.

Max Lucado

We do not understand the intricate pattern of the stars in their course, but we know that He Who created them does, and that just as surely as He guides them, He is charting a safe course for us.

Billy Graham

You may not know what you are going to do; you only know that God knows what He is going to do.

Oswald Chambers

By ourselves we are not capable of suffering bravely, but the Lord possesses all the strength we lack and will demonstrate His power when we undergo persecution.

Corrie ten Boom

A Prayer:

Dear Lord, You rule over our world, and I will allow You to rule over my heart. I will obey Your commandments, I will study Your Word, and I will seek Your will for my life, today and every day of my life. Amen

How should I respond to Jesus' sacrifice on the cross?

The Radical Answer:

Jesus made an incredible sacrifice for you. Now, it's your turn to respond to Christ's sacrifice by turning your heart and your soul over to Him.

Considering the Cross

But as for me, I will never boast about anything except the cross of our Lord Jesus Christ, through whom the world has been crucified to me, and I to the world.

Galatians 6:14 HCSB

As we consider Christ's sacrifice on the cross, we should be profoundly humbled and profoundly grateful. And today, as we come to Christ in prayer, we should do so in a spirit of quiet, heartfelt devotion to the One who gave His life so that we might have life eternal.

He was the Son of God, but He wore a crown of thorns. He was the Savior of mankind, yet He was put to death on a roughhewn cross made of wood. He offered His healing touch to an unsaved world, and yet the same hands that had healed the sick and raised the dead were pierced with nails.

Christ humbled Himself on a cross—for you. He shed His blood—for you. He has offered to walk with you through this life and throughout all eternity. As you approach Him today in prayer, think about His sacrifice and His grace. And be humble.

There is no detour to holiness. Jesus came to the resurrection through the cross, not around it.

Leighton Ford

Come and see the victories of the cross. Christ's wounds are thy healings. His agonies, thy repose. His death, thy life. His sufferings, they salvation.

Matthew Henry

It was not the soldiers who killed him, nor the screams of the mob: It was his devotion to us.

Max Lucado

A Prayer:

Dear Jesus, You are my Savior and my protector. You suffered on the cross for me, and I will give You honor and praise every day of my life. I will honor you with my words, my thoughts, and my prayers. And I will live according to Your commandments, so that through me, others might come to know Your perfect love. Amen

What does the Bible teach us about praising God?

The Radical Answer:

Praise Him! One of the main reasons you and your family go to church is to praise God. But, you need not wait until Sunday rolls around to thank your Heavenly Father. Instead, you can praise Him many times each day by saying silent prayers that only He can hear.

Time to Praise God

I will praise you, Lord, with all my heart. I will tell all the miracles you have done. I will be happy because of you; God Most High, I will sing praises to your name.

Psalm 9:1-2 NCV

When is the best time to praise God? In church? Before dinner is served? When we tuck little children into bed? None of the above. The best time to praise God is all day, every day, to the greatest extent we can, with thanksgiving in our hearts.

Too many of us, even well-intentioned believers, tend to "compartmentalize" our waking hours into a few familiar categories: work, rest, play, family time, and worship. To do so is a mistake. Worship and praise should be woven into the fabric of everything we do; it should never be relegated to a weekly three-hour visit to church on Sunday morning.

Mrs. Charles E. Cowman, the author of the classic devotional text, *Streams in the Desert*, wrote, "Two wings are necessary to lift our souls toward God: prayer and praise. Prayer asks. Praise accepts the answer." Today, find a little more time to lift your concerns to God in prayer, and praise Him for all that He has done. He's listening . . . and He wants to hear from you.

Praise opens the window of our hearts, preparing us to walk more closely with God. Prayer raises the window of our spirit, enabling us to listen more clearly to the Father.

Max Lucado

The Bible instructs—and experience teaches—that praising God results in our burdens being lifted and our joys being multiplied.

Jim Gallery

A Prayer:

Heavenly Father, I come to You today with hope in my heart and praise on my lips. Make me a faithful steward of the blessings You have entrusted to me. Let me follow in Christ's footsteps today and every day that I live. And let my words and deeds praise You now and forever. Amen

What does the Bible say about sin?

The Radical Answer:

Every day of your life, you will be tempted to sin, to rebel against God's teachings. Your job, simply put, is to guard your heart against the darkness as you focus on the light.

Ignoring Sin

For everyone who practices wicked things hates the light and avoids it, so that his deeds may not be exposed. But anyone who lives by the truth comes to the light, so that his works may be shown to be accomplished by God.

John 3:20–21 HCSB

If we deny our sins, we allow those sins to flourish. And if we allow sinful behaviors to become habits, we invite hardships into our own lives and into the lives of our loved ones. When we yield to the distractions and temptations of this troubled world, we suffer. But God has other intentions, and His plans for our lives do not include sin or denial.

When we allow ourselves to encounter God's presence, He will lead us away from temptation, away from confusion, and away from the self-deception. God is the champion of truth and the enemy of denial. May we see ourselves through His eyes and conduct ourselves accordingly.

Man prefers to believe what he prefers to be true.

Francis Bacon

What I like about experience is that it is such an honest thing. You may take any number of wrong turnings; but keep your eyes open and you will not be allowed to go very far before the warning signs appear. You may have deceived yourself, but experience is not trying to deceive you. The universe rings true wherever you fairly test it.

C. S. Lewis

There's none so blind as those who will not see.

Matthew Henry

A Prayer:

Dear Lord, when I displease You, I do injury to myself, to my family, and to my community. Because sin distances me from You, Lord, I will fear sin and I will avoid sinful places. The fear of sinning against You is a healthy fear, Father, because it can motivate me to accomplish Your will. Let a healthy fear of sin guide my path, today and every day of my life. Amen

What does the Bible say about God's love?

The Radical Answer:

When all else fails, God's love does not. You can always depend upon God's love . . . and He is always your ultimate protection.

Embracing God's Love

Unfailing love surrounds those who trust the LORD.

Psalm 32:10 NLT

When we worship God with faith and assurance, and when we place Him at the absolute center of our lives, we invite His love into our hearts. In turn, we grow to love Him more deeply as we sense His love for us. St. Augustine wrote, "I love you, Lord, not doubtingly, but with absolute certainty. Your Word beat upon my heart until I fell in love with you, and now the universe and everything in it tells me to love you." Let us pray that we, too, will turn our hearts to our Heavenly Father, knowing with certainty that He loves us and that we love Him.

God is love, and God's love is perfect. When we open ourselves to His perfect love, we are touched by the Creator's hand, and we are transformed, not just for a day, but for all eternity.

Today, as you carve out quiet moments of thanksgiving and praise for your Heavenly Father, open yourself to His presence and to His love. He is here, waiting. His love is here, always. Accept it—now—and be blessed.

If you have an obedience problem, you have a love problem. Focus your attention on God's love.

Henry Blackaby

Even when we cannot see the why and wherefore of God's dealings, we know that there is love in and behind them, so we can rejoice always.

J. I. Packer

The life of faith is a daily exploration of the constant and countless ways in which God's grace and love are experienced.

Eugene Peterson

A Prayer:

Thank You, Dear God, for Your love. You are my loving Father. I thank You for Your love and for Your Son. I will praise You; I will worship You; and, I will love You today, tomorrow, and forever. Amen

Sometimes, I am afraid. What does the Bible say about fear?

The Radical Answer:

If you're feeling fearful or anxious, you must trust God to solve the problems that are simply too big for you to solve.

Beyond Fear

I sought the Lord, and He answered me and delivered me from all my fears.

Psalm 34:4 HCSB

We live in a world that is, at times, a frightening place. We live in a world that is, at times, a discouraging place. We live in a world where life-changing losses can be so painful and so profound that it seems we will never recover. But, with God's help, and with the help of encouraging family members and friends, we can recover.

During the darker days of life, we are wise to remember the words of Jesus, who reassured His disciples, saying, "Take courage! It is I. Don't be afraid" (Matthew 14:27 NIV). Then, with God's comfort and His love in our hearts, we can offer encouragement to others. And by helping them face their fears, we can, in turn, tackle our own problems with courage, determination, and faith.

When we meditate on God and remember the promises He has given us in His Word, our faith grows, and our fears dissolve.

Charles Stanley

The Lord Jesus by His Holy Spirit is with me, and the knowledge of His presence dispels the darkness and allays any fears.

Bill Bright

One of the main missions of God is to free us from the debilitating bonds of fear and anxiety. God's heart is broken when He sees us so demoralized and weighed down by fear.

Bill Hybels

When we submit difficult and alarming situations to God, he promises that his peace will be like a military garrison to guard our hearts from fear.

Dennis Swanberg

A Prayer:

Your Word reminds me, Lord, that even when I walk through the valley of the shadow of death, I need fear no evil, for You are with me, and You comfort me. Thank You, Lord, for a perfect love that casts out fear. Let me live courageously and faithfully this day and every day. Amen

There's so much to learn. How can my family and I keep up with it all?

The Radical Answer:

Simple: you've got to keep learning and growing every day. And remember the advice of centenarian Marie T. Freeman: "Stay interested in everything and everybody. It keeps you young."

Lifetime Learning

Start with God—the first step in learning is bowing down to God.

Proverbs 1:7 MSG

Whether you're twenty-two or a hundred and two, you've still got lots to learn. Even if you're a very wise man, God isn't finished with you yet, and He isn't finished teaching you important lessons about life here on earth and life eternal.

Do you seek to live a life of righteousness and wisdom? If so, you must continue to study the ultimate source of wisdom: the Word of God. You must associate, day in and day out, with godly men and women. And, you must act in accordance with your beliefs. When you study God's Word and live according to His commandments, you will become wise . . . and you will be a blessing to your friends, to your family, and to the world.

The wonderful thing about God's schoolroom is that we get to grade our own papers. You see, He doesn't test us so He can learn how well we're doing. He tests us so we can discover how well we're doing.

Charles Swindoll

Knowledge is power.

Francis Bacon

The wise man gives proper appreciation in his life to this past. He learns to sift the sawdust of heritage in order to find the nuggets that make the current moment have any meaning.

Grady Nutt

It's the things you learn after you know it all that really count.

Vance Havner

A Prayer:

Dear Lord, I have so much to learn. Help me to watch, to listen, to think, and to learn, every day of my life. Amen

Everybody (including me) has problems. What can God's Word teach me about my problems?

The Radical Answer:

When it comes to solving problems, work beats worry. Remember: It is better to fix than to fret.

Problem-solving 101

People who do what is right may have many problems, but the Lord will solve them all.

Psalm 34:19 NCV

Life is an adventure in problem-solving. The question is not whether we will encounter problems; the real question is how we will choose to address them. When it comes to solving the problems of everyday living, we often know precisely what needs to be done, but we may be slow in doing it—especially if what needs to be done is difficult. So we put off till tomorrow what should be done today.

As a man living here in the 21st-century, you have your own set of challenges. As you face those challenges, you may be comforted by this fact: Trouble, of every kind, is temporary. Yet God's grace is eternal. And worries, of every kind, are temporary. But God's love is everlasting. The troubles that concern you will pass. God remains. And for every problem, God has a solution.

The words of Psalm 34 remind us that the Lord solves problems for "people who do what is right." And usually, doing "what is right" means doing the uncomfortable work of confronting our problems sooner rather than later. So with no further ado, let the problem-solving begin . . . right now.

Life will be made or broken at the place where we meet and deal with obstacles.

E. Stanley Jones

Each problem is a God-appointed instructor.

Charles Swindoll

I choose joy. I will refuse the temptation to be cynical; cynicism is the tool of a lazy thinker. I will refuse to see people as anything less than human beings, created by God. I will refuse to see any problem as anything less than an opportunity to see God.

Max Lucado

A Prayer:

Lord, sometimes my problems are simply too big for me, but they are never too big for You. Let me turn my troubles over to You, Lord, and let me trust in You today and for all eternity. Amen

Sometimes, I can be overly critical of my family members. What does the Bible say about that?

The Radical Answer:

If you're tempted to be critical of others, remember that you must treat others in the way you want to be treated. So do everybody (including yourself) a favor: don't be overly critical. And husbands beware: You cannot pursue intimacy with God while demeaning your wife. So you must never, never, never demean your wife for any reason. Never.

Critics Beware

Don't criticize one another, brothers. He who criticizes a brother or judges his brother criticizes the law and judges the law. But if you judge the law, you are not a doer of the law but a judge.

James 4:11 HCSB

From experience, we know that it is easier to criticize than to correct; we understand that it is easier to find faults than solutions; and we realize that excessive criticism is usually destructive, not productive. Yet the urge to criticize others remains a powerful temptation for most of us. Our task, as obedient believers, is to break the twin habits of negative thinking and critical speech.

Negativity is highly contagious: we give it to others who, in turn, give it back to us. This cycle can be broken by positive thoughts, heartfelt prayers, and encouraging words. As thoughtful servants of a loving God, we can use the transforming power of Christ's love to break the chains of negativity. And we should.

We shall never come to the perfect man til we come to the perfect world.

Matthew Henry

Being critical of others, including God, is one way we try to avoid facing and judging our own sins.

Warren Wiersbe

After one hour in heaven, we shall be ashamed that we ever grumbled.

Vance Havner

A Prayer:

Help me, Lord, rise above the need to criticize others. May my own shortcomings humble me, and may I always be a source of genuine encouragement to my family and friends. Amen

What's the best way for me to communicate my beliefs to my loved ones?

The Radical Answer:

By your words and your example. And the greatest of these is example.

Your Beliefs

Do what God's teaching says; when you only listen and do nothing, you are fooling yourselves.

James 1:22 NCV

In describing one's beliefs, actions are far better descriptors than words. Yet far too many of us spend more energy talking about our beliefs than living by them—with predictable consequences.

Is your life a picture book of your creed? Are your actions congruent with your beliefs? Are you willing to practice the philosophy that you preach?

Today and every day, make certain that your actions are guided by God's Word and by the conscience that He has placed in your heart. Don't treat your faith as if it were separate from your everyday life. Weave your beliefs into the very fabric of your day. When you do, God will honor your good works, and your good works will honor God.

Once you have thoroughly examined your values and articulated them, you will be able to steer your life by them.

John Maxwell

Believe and do what God says. The life-changing consequences will be limitless, and the results will be confidence and peace of mind.

Franklin Graham

God calls us to be committed to Him, to be committed to making a difference, and to be committed to reconciliation.

Bill Hybels

The reason many of us do not ardently believe in the gospel is that we have never given it a rigorous testing, thrown our hard questions at it, or faced it with our most prickly doubts.

Eugene Peterson

A Prayer:

Heavenly Father, I believe in You, and I believe in Your Word. Help me to live in such a way that my actions validate my beliefs—and let the glory be Yours forever. Amen

What does the Bible say about fearing God?

The Radical Answer:

It's simple: If you have a healthy fear of God, you're wise—if you don't, you're not.

The Right Kind of Fear

A simple life in the Fear-of-God is better than a rich life with a ton of headaches.

Proverbs 15:16 MSG

God's hand shapes the universe, and it shapes our lives. God maintains absolute sovereignty over His creation, and His power is beyond comprehension. As believers, we must cultivate a sincere respect for God's awesome power. God has dominion over all things, and until we acknowledge His sovereignty, we lack the humility we need to live righteously, and we lack the humility we need to become wise.

The fear of the Lord is, indeed, the beginning of knowledge. So today, as you face the realities of everyday life, remember this: until you acquire a healthy, respectful fear of God's power, your education is incomplete, and so is your faith.

The remarkable thing about fearing God is that when you fear God, you fear nothing else, whereas if you do not fear God, you fear everything else.

Oswald Chambers

When true believers are awed by the greatness of God and by the privilege of becoming His children, then they become sincerely motivated, effective evangelists.

Bill Hybels

A healthy fear of God will do much to deter us from sin.

Charles Swindoll

The fear of God is the death of every other fear.

C. H. Spurgeon

A Prayer:

Lord, you love me and protect me. I praise You, Father, for Your grace, and I respect You for Your infinite power. Let my greatest fear in life be the fear of displeasing You. Amen

I want to sense a calling from God. What does the Bible say about that?

The Radical Answer:

If you ask God for His guidance, He will give it (John 10:10). And then, when you sense God's leading, your responsibility is clear: to answer His call.

Answering the Call

God chose you to be his people, so I urge you now to live the life to which God called you.

Ephesians 4:1 NCV

It is vitally important that you heed God's call. In John 15:16, Jesus says, "You did not choose me, but I chose you and appointed you to go and bear fruit—fruit that will last" (NIV). In other words, you have been called by Christ, and now, it is up to you to decide precisely how you will answer.

Have you already found your special calling? If so, you're a very lucky guy. If not, keep searching and keep praying until you discover it. And remember this: God has important work for you to do—work that no one else on earth can accomplish but you.

The world does not consider labor a blessing, therefore it flees and hates it, but the pious who fear the Lord labor with a ready and cheerful heart, for they know God's command, and they acknowledge His calling.

Martin Luther

When you become consumed by God's call on your life, everything will take on new meaning and significance. You will begin to see every facet of your life, including your pain, as a means through which God can work to bring others to Himself.

Charles Stanley

God never calls without enabling us. In other words, if he calls you to do something, he makes it possible for you to do it.

Luci Swindoll

A Prayer:

Heavenly Father, You have called me, and I acknowledge that calling. In these quiet moments before this busy day unfolds, I come to You. I will study Your Word and seek Your guidance. Give me the wisdom to know Your will for my life and the courage to follow wherever You may lead me, today and forever. Amen

Sometimes, I become discouraged, and sometimes I'm worried. What should I do?

The Radical Answer:

If you believe the promises contained in God's Word, your future—and your family's future—is secure. So when you consider God's blessings, you should be thankful, optimistic, and ready to serve.

Watching the Donut

I can do everything through him that gives me strength.

Philippians 4:13 NIV

On the wall of a little donut shop, the sign said:

As you travel through life, brother,

Whatever be your goal,

Keep your eye upon the donut,

And not upon the hole.

Are you a Christian who keeps your eye upon the donut, or have you acquired the bad habit of looking only at the hole? Hopefully, you spend most of your waking hours looking at the donut (and thanking God for it).

Christianity and pessimism don't mix. So do yourself a favor: choose to be a hope-filled Christian. Think optimistically about your life and your future. Trust your hopes, not your fears. Take time to celebrate God's glorious creation. And then, when you've filled your heart with hope and gladness, share your optimism with your friends. They'll be better for it, and so will you. But not necessarily in that order.

The people whom I have seen succeed best in life have always been cheerful and hopeful people who went about their business with a smile on their faces.

Charles Kingsley

The essence of optimism is that it takes no account of the present, but it is a source of inspiration, of vitality, and of hope. Where others have resigned, it enables a man to hold his head high, to claim the future for himself, and not abandon it to his enemy.

Dietrich Bonhoeffer

A Prayer:

Lord, let me be an expectant Christian. Let me expect the best from You, and let me look for the best in others. If I become discouraged, Father, turn my thoughts and my prayers to You. Let me trust You, Lord, to direct my life. And, let me share my faith and optimism with others, today and every day that I live. Amen

What does the Bible teach us about worship?

The Radical Answer:

The best way for you and your family to worship God is to worship Him sincerely and often.

Family Worship

Worship the Lord with gladness. Come before him, singing with joy. Acknowledge that the Lord is God! He made us, and we are his. We are his people, the sheep of his pasture.

Psalm 100:2-3 NLT

All of mankind is engaged in the practice of worship. Some choose to worship God and, as a result, reap the joy that He intends for His children. Others distance themselves from God by worshiping such things as earthly possessions or personal gratification and when they do so, they suffer.

Today, make every aspect of your life a cause for celebration and worship. Praise God for the blessings and opportunities that He has given you, and live according to the beautiful words found in the 5th chapter of 1 Thessalonians: "Rejoice evermore. Pray without ceasing. In every thing give thanks: for this is the will of God in Christ Jesus concerning you" (vv. 16-18). God deserves your worship, your prayers, your praise, and your thanks. And, you deserve the joy that is yours when you worship Him with your prayers, your deeds, and your life.

Each of us needs a place of worship, such as our church. We need a place we can be reminded of God's word and a place where we can revere His presence. Primarily, though, we worship in spirit, in the sanctuary of the heart.

Franklin Graham

Worship is an act which develops feelings for God, not a feeling for God which is expressed in an act of worship. When we obey the command to praise God in worship, our deep, essential need to be in relationship with God is nurtured.

Eugene Peterson

When God is at the center of your life, you worship. When he's not, you worry.

Rick Warren

A Prayer:

Heavenly Father, let today and every day be a time of worship for me and my family. Let us worship You, not only with words, but also with deeds. In the quiet moments of the day, let us praise You and thank You for creating us, loving us, guiding us, and saving us. Amen

What does the Bible say about physical fitness?

The Radical Answer:

God's Word teaches that your body is a miraculous gift from the Creator, and you should treat it that way.

Fitness Matters

Whatever you eat or drink or whatever you do, you must do all for the glory of God.

1 Corinthians 10:31 NLT

Are you shaping up or spreading out? Do you eat sensibly and exercise regularly, or do you spend most of your time on the couch with a Twinkie in one hand and a clicker in the other? Are you choosing to treat your body like a temple or a trash heap? How you answer these questions will help determine how long you live and how well you live.

Physical fitness is a choice, a choice that requires discipline—it's as simple as that. So, do yourself this favor: treat your body like a one-of-a-kind gift from God . . . because that's precisely what your body is.

If you desire to improve your physical well-being and your emotional outlook, increasing your faith can help you.

John Maxwell

Jesus Christ is the One by Whom, for Whom, through Whom everything was made. Therefore, He knows what's wrong in your life and how to fix it.

Anne Graham Lotz

A Christian should no more defile his body than a Jew would defile the temple.

Warren Wiersbe

Our primary motivation should not be for more energy or to avoid a heart attack but to please God with our bodies.

Carole Lewis

A Prayer:

Dear Lord, my body is Your temple—I will treat it with care. Amen

At times, I feel discontented with life. How can I find lasting contentment?

The Radical Answer:

Contentment comes, not from your circumstances, but from your attitude.

Genuine Contentment

I have learned to be content in whatever circumstances I am.

Philippians 4:11 HCSB

The preoccupation with happiness and contentment is an ever-present theme in the modern world. We are bombarded with messages that tell us where to find peace and pleasure in a world that worships materialism and wealth. But, lasting contentment is not found in material possessions; genuine contentment is a spiritual gift from God to those who trust in Him and follow His commandments.

Where can you and your family members find contentment? If you don't find it in God, you will never find it anywhere else. But, if you put your faith and your trust in Him, you will be blessed with an inner peace that is beyond human understanding. When God dwells at the center of your lives, peace and contentment will belong to you just as surely as you belong to God.

He is truly happy who has all that he wishes to have, and wishes to have nothing that he ought not to have.

St. Augustine

Contentment is difficult because nothing on earth can satisfy our deepest longing. We long to see God.

Max Lucado

Contentment is not escape from battle, but rather an abiding peace and confidence in the midst of battle.

Warren Wiersbe

Real contentment hinges on what's happening inside us, not around us.

Charles Stanley

A Prayer:

Dear Lord, You offer me contentment and peace; let me accept Your peace. Help me to trust Your Word, to follow Your commandments, and to welcome the peace of Jesus into my heart, today and forever. Amen

When I displease God or injure other people, what can I do? How can I make things right with God?

The Radical Answer:

If you're engaged in behavior that is displeasing to God, today is the day to stop. First, confess your sins to God. Then, ask Him what actions you should take in order to make things right again.

Real Repentance

The one who conceals his sins will not prosper, but whoever confesses and renounces them will find mercy.

Proverbs 28:13 HCSB

Who among us has sinned? All of us. But, God calls upon us to turn away from sin by following His commandments. And the good news is this: When we do ask God's forgiveness and turn our hearts to Him, He forgives us absolutely and completely.

Genuine repentance requires more than simply offering God apologies for our misdeeds. Real repentance may start with feelings of sorrow and remorse, but it ends only when we turn away from the sin that has heretofore distanced us from our Creator. In truth, we offer our most meaningful apologies to God, not with our words, but with our actions. As long as we are still engaged in sin, we may be "repenting," but we have not fully "repented."

Is there an aspect of your life that is distancing you from your God? If so, ask for His forgiveness, and—just as importantly—stop sinning. Then, wrap yourself in the protection of God's Word. When you do, you will be secure.

Repentance begins with confession of our guilt and recognition that our sin is against God.

Charles Stanley

Ten thousand confessions, if they do not spring from really contrite hearts, shall only be additions to their guilt.

C. H. Spurgeon

A Prayer:

When I stray from Your commandments, Lord, I must not only confess my sins, I must also turn from them. When I fall short, help me to change. When I reject Your Word and Your will for my life, guide me back to Your side. Forgive my sins, Dear Lord, and help me live according to Your plan for my life. Your plan is perfect, Father; I am not. Let me trust in You. Amen

I'm a very busy person with a very full to-do list. What should I do?

The Radical Answer:

Do first things first, and keep your focus on high-priority tasks. And remember this: your highest priority should be your relationship with God and His Son.

Too Busy?

Come to Me, all you who are weary and burdened, and I will give you rest. Take My yoke upon you and learn from Me, because I am gentle and humble in heart, and you will find rest for your souls. For My yoke is easy and My burden is light.

Matthew 11:28-30 HCSB

Has the busy pace of life robbed you of the peace that might otherwise be yours through Jesus Christ? If so, you are simply too busy for your own good. Through His Son Jesus, God offers you a peace that passes human understanding, but He won't force His peace upon you; in order to experience it, you must slow down long enough to sense His presence and His love.

Today, as a gift to yourself, to your family, and to the world, slow down and claim the inner peace that is your spiritual birthright: the peace of Jesus Christ. It is offered freely; it has been paid for in full; it is yours for the asking. So ask. And then share.

Being busy, in and of itself, is not a sin. But being busy in an endless pursuit of things that leave us empty and hollow and broken inside—that cannot be pleasing to God.

Max Lucado

This is a day when we are so busy doing everything that we have no time to be anything. Even religiously we are so occupied with activities that we have no time to know God.

Vance Havner

The foe of opportunity is preoccupation. Just when God sends along a chance to turn a great victory for mankind, some of us are too busy puttering around to notice it.

A. W. Tozer

A Prayer:

Dear Lord, sometimes, I am distracted by the busyness of the day or the demands of the moment. When I am worried or anxious, Father, turn my thoughts back to You. Help me to trust Your will, to follow Your commands, and to accept Your peace, today and forever. Amen

What does God's Word say about God's Son?

The Radical Answer:

What a friend you have in Jesus! Jesus loves you, and He offers you eternal life with Him in heaven. Welcome Him into your heart. Now!

What a Friend

Therefore if any man be in Christ, he is a new creature: old things are passed away; behold, all things are become new.

2 Corinthians 5:17 KJV

Our circumstances change but Jesus does not. Even when the world seems to be trembling between our feet, Jesus remains the spiritual bedrock that cannot be moved.

The old familiar hymn begins, "What a friend we have in Jesus…." No truer words were ever penned. Jesus is the sovereign Friend and ultimate Savior of mankind. Christ showed enduring love for His believers by willingly sacrificing His own life so that we might have eternal life. Let us love Him, praise Him, and share His message of salvation with our neighbors and with the world.

Jesus came into the world so we could know, once and for all, that God is concerned about the way we live, the way we believe, and the way we die.

Billy Graham

Jesus: the proof of God's love.

Philip Yancey

Jesus was the perfect reflection of God's nature in every situation He encountered during His time here on earth.

Bill Hybels

Jesus is the personal approach from the unseen God coming so near that he becomes inescapable. You don't have to find him—you just have to consent to be found.

E. Stanley Jones

A Prayer:

Heavenly Father, I praise You for Your Son. Jesus is my Savior and my strength. Let me share His Good News with all who cross my path, and let me share His love with all who need His healing touch. Amen

Sometimes it's hard to be an obedient Christian. What does the Bible say about obedience?

The Radical Answer:

God rewards obedience and punishes disobedience. It's not enough to understand God's rules; you must also live by them or face the consequences.

Obedience Now

Not everyone who says to Me, "Lord, Lord!" will enter the kingdom of heaven, but the one who does the will of My Father in heaven.

Matthew 7:21 HCSB

God's laws are eternal and unchanging: obedience leads to abundance and joy; disobedience leads to disaster. God has given us a guidebook for righteous living called the Holy Bible. If we trust God's Word and live by it, we are blessed. But, if we choose to ignore God's commandments, the results are as predictable as they are tragic.

Life is a series of decisions and choices. Each day, we make countless decisions that can bring us closer to God... or not. When we live according to God's commandments, we earn for ourselves the abundance and peace that He intends for our lives.

Do you seek God's peace and His blessings? Then obey Him. When you're faced with a difficult choice or a powerful temptation, seek God's counsel and trust the counsel He gives. Invite God into your heart and live according to His commandments. When you do, you will be blessed today, and tomorrow, and forever.

Believe and do what God says. The life-changing consequences will be limitless, and the results will be confidence and peace of mind.

Franklin Graham

All true knowledge of God is born out of obedience.

John Calvin

Obedience is the outward expression of your love of God.

Henry Blackaby

A Prayer:

Lord, my family is both a priceless gift and a profound responsibility. Let my actions be worthy of that responsibility. Lead me along Your path, Lord, and guide me far from the frustrations and distractions of this troubled world. Let Your Holy Word guide my actions, and let Your love reside in my heart, this day and every day. Amen

What does the Bible say about family life?

The Radical Answer:

Your family is God's gift to you. Let your family members know that you love them by the things you say and the things you do. And, never take your family for granted; they deserve your attention, your care, and your support.

Caring for Your Family

Whoever does not care for his own relatives, especially his own family members, has turned against the faith and is worse than someone who does not believe in God.

1 Timothy 5:8 NCV

The words of 1 Timothy 5:8 are unambiguous: if God has blessed us with families, then He expects us to care for them. Sometimes, this profound responsibility seems daunting. And sometimes, even for the most dedicated Christian men, family life holds moments of frustration and disappointment. But, for those who are lucky enough to live in the presence of a close-knit, caring clan, the rewards far outweigh the demands.

No family is perfect, and neither is yours. Despite the inevitable challenges of providing for your family, and despite the occasional hurt feelings of family life, your clan is

God's gift to you. Give thanks to the Giver for the gift of family . . . and act accordingly.

It is a reverent thing to see an ancient castle or building not in decay, or to see a fair timber tree sound and perfect. How much more beautiful it is to behold an ancient and noble family that has stood against the waves and weathers of time.

Francis Bacon

Never give your family the leftovers and crumbs of your time.

Charles Swindoll

The only true source of meaning in life is found in love for God and his son Jesus Christ, and love for mankind, beginning with our own families.

James Dobson

A Prayer:

Lord, You have given me a family to love and to care for. Thank You, Father. I will love all the members of my family despite their imperfections. Let them love me, Dear Lord, despite mine. Amen

What does the Bible say about the need to share my personal testimony with family and friends?

The Radical Answer:

If your eternity with God is secure (because you've given your heart to Jesus), you have a profound responsibility to tell as many people as you can about the eternal life that Christ offers to those who believe in Him. And, of course, it's up to you to make sure that your family members know where you stand.

Sharing Your Faith

But sanctify the Lord God in your hearts, and always be ready to give a defense to everyone who asks you a reason for the hope that is in you.

1 Peter 3:15 HCSB

Our personal testimonies are extremely important, but sometimes, because of shyness or insecurities, we're afraid to share our experiences. And that's unfortunate.

In his second letter to Timothy, Paul shares a message to believers of every generation when he writes, "God has not given us a spirit of timidity" (1:7). Paul's meaning is clear: When sharing our beliefs, we, as Christians, must be courageous, forthright, and unashamed.

We live in a world that desperately needs the healing message of Christ Jesus. Every believer, each in his or her own way, bears responsibility for sharing the Good News of our Savior.

Billy Graham observed, "Our faith grows by expression. If we want to keep our faith, we must share it." If you are a follower of Christ, the time to express your belief in Him is now. You know how He has touched your heart; help Him do the same for others.

To take up the cross means that you take your stand for the Lord Jesus no matter what it costs.

Billy Graham

To stand in an uncaring world and say, "See, here is the Christ" is a daring act of courage.

Calvin Miller

A Prayer:

Lord, the life that I live and the words that I speak will tell my family and the world how I feel about You. Today and every day, let my testimony be worthy of You. Let my words be sure and true, and let my actions point others to You. Amen

Sometimes, it's easy to think, "I've done that," when it was, in truth, God who did it. So what does the Bible say about humility?

The Radical Answer:

God favors the humble just as surely as He disciplines the proud. So you must remain humble or face the consequences. Pride does go before the fall, but humility often prevents the fall.

The Wisdom to Be Humble

God has chosen you and made you his holy people. He loves you. So always do these things: Show mercy to others, be kind, humble, gentle, and patient.

Colossians 3:12 NCV

When we experience success, it's easy to puff out our chests and proclaim, "I did that!" But it's wrong. Dietrich Bonhoeffer was correct when he observed, "It is very easy to overestimate the importance of our own achievements in comparison with what we owe others." In other words, reality breeds humility.

Who are the greatest among us? Are they the proud and the powerful? Hardly. The greatest among us are the humble servants who care less for their own glory and more for God's glory. If we seek greatness in God's eyes, we must forever praise God's good works, not our own.

If you're tempted to overestimate your own accomplishments, resist that temptation. Instead of puffing out your chest and saying, "Look at me!", give credit where credit is due, starting with God. And, rest assured: There is no such thing as a self-made man. All of us are made by God...and He deserves the glory, not us.

God exalts humility. When God works in our lives, helping us to become humble, he gives us a permanent joy. Humility gives us a joy that cannot be taken away.

Max Lucado

It was pride that changed angels into devils; it is humility that makes men as angels.

St. Augustine

A Prayer:

Heavenly Father, Jesus clothed Himself with humility when He chose to leave heaven and come to earth to live and die for all creation. Christ is my Master and my example. Clothe me with humility, Lord, so that I might be more like Your Son. Amen

The Bible makes many promises. Can I depend upon those promises?

The Radical Answer:

Yes! God is always faithful and His Word endures forever. So you and your family should study God's Word (every day) and trust it. When you do, you will be blessed.

He Keeps His Promises

Let us hold on to the confession of our hope without wavering, for He who promised is faithful.

Hebrews 10:23 HCSB

God has made quite a few promises to you, and He intends to keep every single one of them. You will find these promises in a book like no other: the Holy Bible. The Bible is your roadmap for life here on earth and for life eternal—as a believer, you are called upon to trust its promises, to follow its commandments, and to share its Good News.

God has made promises to all of humanity and to you. God's promises never fail and they never grow old. You must trust those promises and share them with your family, with your friends, and with the world . . . starting now . . . and ending never.

There are four words I wish we would never forget, and they are, "God keeps his word."

Charles Swindoll

The stars may fall, but God's promises will stand and be fulfilled.

J. I. Packer

God's promises are overflowings from his great heart.

C. H. Spurgeon

The promises of Scripture are not mere pious hopes or sanctified guesses. They are more than sentimental words to be printed on decorated cards for Sunday School children. They are eternal verities. They are true. There is no perhaps about them.

Peter Marshall

A Prayer:

Lord, Your Holy Word contains promises, and I will trust them. I will use the Bible as my guide, and I will trust You, Lord, to speak to me through Your Holy Spirit and through Your Holy Word, this day and forever. Amen

We live in a noisy world where it's hard to find a moment's peace. What does the Bible teach us about peace?

The Radical Answer:

God's peace surpasses human understanding. When you accept His peace, it will revolutionize your life.

Accepting His Peace

And the peace of God, which surpasses all comprehension, will guard your hearts and your minds in Christ Jesus.

Philippians 4:7 NASB

As a busy person, your plate is probably full: work to do, bills to pay, a family to lead. Sometimes it seems that you can scarcely find a moment's peace. But the beautiful words of John 14:27 are a reminder that God's peace is always available to you.

Jesus said, "Peace I leave with you, my peace I give unto you . . . ." Christ offers us peace, not as the world gives, but as He alone gives. We, as believers, can accept His peace or ignore it.

When we accept the peace of Jesus Christ into our hearts, our lives are transformed. And then, because we possess the gift of peace, we can share that gift with fellow Christians, family members, friends, and associates. If, on the other hand, we choose to ignore the gift of peace—for whatever reason—we simply cannot share what we do not possess.

Today, as a gift to yourself, to your family, and to your friends, claim the inner peace that is your spiritual birthright: the peace of Jesus Christ. It is offered freely; it has been paid for in full; it is yours for the asking. So ask. And then share.

A great many people are trying to make peace, but that has already been done. God has not left it for us to do; all we have to do is to enter into it.

D. L. Moody

That peace, which has been described and which believers enjoy, is a participation of the peace which their glorious Lord and Master himself enjoys.

Jonathan Edwards

A Prayer:

Dear Lord, the peace that the world offers is fleeting, but You offer a peace that is perfect and eternal. Let me take my concerns and burdens to You, Father, and let me feel the spiritual abundance that You offer through the person of Your Son, the Prince of Peace. Amen

I want to sense God's presence. What should I do?

The Radical Answer:

God isn't far away—He's right here, right now. And He's willing to talk to you right here, right now. So find a quiet place and open your heart to Him. When you do, you'll sense God's presence and His love, which, by the way, is already surrounding you and your loved ones.

He's Here

I am not alone, because the Father is with Me.

John 16:32 HCSB

Where is God? God is eternally with us. He is omnipresent. He is, quite literally, everywhere you have ever been and everywhere you will ever go. He is with you night and day; He knows your every thought; He hears your every heartbeat.

Sometimes, in the crush of your daily duties, God may seem far away. Or sometimes, when the disappointments and sorrows of life leave you brokenhearted, God may seem distant, but He is not. When you earnestly seek God, you will find Him because He is here, waiting patiently for you to reach out to Him . . . right here . . . right now.

There is a basic urge: the longing for unity. You desire a reunion with God—with God your Father.

E. Stanley Jones

The next time you hear a baby laugh or see an ocean wave, take note. Pause and listen as his Majesty whispers ever so gently, "I'm here."

Max Lucado

Get yourself into the presence of the loving Father. Just place yourself before Him, and look up into, His face; think of His love, His wonderful, tender, pitying love.

Andrew Murray

God is at work; He is in full control; He is in the midst of whatever has happened, is happening, and will happen.

Charles Swindoll

A Prayer:

Dear Lord, You are with me always. Help me feel Your presence in every situation and every circumstance. Today, Dear God, let me feel You and acknowledge Your presence, Your love, and Your Son. Amen

I learned the Golden Rule as a child, but now that I'm an adult, what should it mean to me?

The Radical Answer:
The Golden Rule applies to all believers of all ages, including you. That means that you must strive to treat other people—all people—in the same way you want to be treated. No exceptions.

His Golden Rule

Do to others as you would have them do to you.

Luke 6:31 NIV

Some rules are easier to understand than they are to live by. Jesus told us that we should treat other people in the same way that we want to be treated: that's the Golden Rule. But sometimes, especially when we're feeling pressure from friends, or when we're tired or upset, obeying the Golden Rule can seem like an impossible task—but it's not.

God wants us to treat other people with respect, kindness, and courtesy. He wants us to rise above our own imperfections, and He wants us to treat others with unselfishness and love. To make it short and sweet, God wants us to obey the Golden Rule, and He knows we can do it.

So if you're wondering how to treat someone else, ask the person you see every time you look into the mirror. The answer you receive will tell you exactly what to do.

The mark of a Christian is that he will walk the second mile and turn the other cheek. A wise man or woman gives the extra effort, all for the glory of the Lord Jesus Christ.

John Maxwell

When you extend hospitality to others, you're not trying to impress people, you're trying to reflect God to them.

Max Lucado

Faith never asks whether good works are to be done, but has done them before there is time to ask the question, and it is always doing them.

Martin Luther

A Prayer:

Dear Lord, let me treat others as I wish to be treated. Because I expect kindness, let me be kind. Because I wish to be loved, let me be loving. Because I need forgiveness, let me be merciful. In all things, Lord, let me live by the Golden Rule that is the commandment of Your Son Jesus. Amen

Sometimes, when I'm supposed to be having fun, I feel guilty. What does the Bible say about fun?

The Radical Answer:

Today and every day, God wants you to rejoice. In fact, He teaches us that every day is a cause for celebration: So don't feel guilty about having good, clean fun. As long as you're following in the footsteps of His Son, God approves.

Time for Fun

So I recommend having fun, because there is nothing better for people to do in this world than to eat, drink, and enjoy life. That way they will experience some happiness along with all the hard work God gives them.

Ecclesiastes 8:15 NLT

Are you a man who takes time each day to really enjoy life? Hopefully so. After all, you are the recipient of a precious gift—the gift of life. And because God has seen fit to give you this gift, it is incumbent upon you to use it and to enjoy it. But sometimes, amid the inevitable pressures of everyday living, really enjoying life may seem almost impossible. It is not.

For most of us, fun is as much a function of attitude as it is a function of environment. So whether you're standing victorious atop one of life's mountains or trudging through one of life's valleys, enjoy yourself. You deserve to have fun today, and God wants you to have fun today . . . so what on earth are you waiting for?

If we don't hunger and thirst after righteousness, we'll become anemic and feel miserable in our Christian experience.

Franklin Graham

True happiness and contentment cannot come from the things of this world. The blessedness of true joy is a free gift that comes only from our Lord and Savior, Jesus Christ.

Dennis Swanberg

The happiest people in the world are not those who have no problems, but the people who have learned to live with those things that are less than perfect.

James Dobson

A Prayer:

Dear Lord, I will rejoice in the countless blessings that You have given me. Let me be a happy Christian, Father, as I share the Good News of Your Son, and let me praise You for all the marvelous things You have done. Amen

What does the Bible have to say about happiness?

The Radical Answer:

Jesus intends for our joy to be complete (John 15:11). And He came to earth so that we might experience His abundance (John 10:10). So, if we're wise, we'll open our hearts to Christ and celebrate His gifts today, tomorrow, and forever.

A Happy Christian

Happy are the people whose strength is in You, whose hearts are set on pilgrimage.

Psalm 84:5 HCSB

Happiness depends less upon our circumstances than upon our thoughts. When we turn our thoughts to God, to His gifts, and to His glorious creation, we experience the joy that God intends for His children. But, when we focus on the negative aspects of life, we suffer needlessly.

Do you sincerely want to be a happy Christian? Then set your mind and your heart upon God's love and His grace. The fullness of life in Christ is available to all who seek it and claim it. Count yourself among that number. Seek first the salvation that is available through a personal relationship with Jesus Christ, and then claim the joy, the peace, and the spiritual abundance that the Shepherd offers His sheep.

There is no correlation between wealth and happiness.

Larry Burkett

Our thoughts, not our circumstances, determine our happiness.

John Maxwell

Whoever possesses God is happy.

St. Augustine

God has charged Himself with full responsibility for our eternal happiness and stands ready to take over the management of our lives the moment we turn in faith to Him.

A. W. Tozer

A Prayer:

Dear Lord, You are my strength and my joy. I will rejoice in the day that You have made, and I will give thanks for the countless blessings that You have given me. Let me be a joyful Christian, Father, as I share Your Good News with friends, with family, and with the world. Amen

I can be very hard on myself at times. What does the Bible say about my self-worth?

The Radical Answer:

Don't worry too much about self-worth: Instead, worry more about living a life that is pleasing to God. Learn to think optimistically. Find a worthy purpose. Find people to love and people to serve. When you do, your self-worth will, on most days, take care of itself.

Your Own Worst Critic?

Those who wait for perfect weather will never plant seeds; those who look at every cloud will never harvest crops. . . . Plant early in the morning, and work until evening, because you don't know if this or that will succeed. They might both do well.

Ecclesiastes 11:4, 6 NCV

When God made you, He equipped you with an array of talents and abilities that are uniquely yours. It's up to you to discover those talents and to use them, but sometimes your own perfectionism may get in the way.

If you're your own worst critic, give it up. After all, God doesn't expect you to be perfect, and if that's okay with Him, then it should be okay with you, too.

When you accepted Christ as your Savior, God accepted you for all eternity. Now, it's your turn to accept yourself. When you do, you'll feel a tremendous weight being lifted from your shoulders. And that's as it should be. After all, only one earthly being ever lived life to perfection, and He was the Son of God. The rest of us have fallen short of God's standard and need to be accepting of our own limitations as well as the limitations of others.

The happiest people in the world are not those who have no problems, but the people who have learned to live with those things that are less than perfect.

James Dobson

What makes a Christian a Christian is not perfection but forgiveness.

Max Lucado

A Prayer:

Lord, this world has so many expectations of me, but today I will not seek to meet the world's expectations; I will do my best to meet Your expectations. I will make You my ultimate priority, Lord, by serving You, by praising You, by loving You, and by obeying You. Amen

I would like to believe that I am protected by God. What does the Bible say about that?

The Radical Answer:

You are protected by God . . . now and always. Earthly security is an illusion. Your only real security comes from the loving heart of God.

The Ultimate Armor

If God is for us, who is against us?

Romans 8:31 HCSB

God has promised to protect us, and He intends to keep His promise. In a world filled with dangers and temptations, God is the ultimate armor. In a world filled with misleading messages, God's Word is the ultimate truth. In a world filled with more frustrations than we can count, God's Son offers the ultimate peace.

Will you accept God's peace and wear God's armor against the dangers of our world? Hopefully so—because when you do, you can live courageously, knowing that you possess the ultimate protection: God's unfailing love for you.

The Rock of Ages is the great sheltering encirclement.

Oswald Chambers

Under heaven's lock and key, we are protected by the most efficient security system available: the power of God.

Charles Swindoll

A mighty fortress is our God, a bulwark never failing / Our helper He, amid the flood of mortal ills prevailing / For still our ancient foe doth seek to work us woe / His craft and power are great, armed with cruel hate, / Our earth is not his equal.

Martin Luther

As sure as God puts his children in the furnace, he will be in the furnace with them.

C. H. Spurgeon

A Prayer:

Lord, sometimes life is difficult. Sometimes, I am worried, weary, or heartbroken. And sometimes, I encounter powerful temptations to disobey Your commandments. But, when I lift my eyes to You, Father, You strengthen me. When I am weak, You lift me up. Today, I will turn to You for strength, for hope, for direction, and for deliverance. Amen

It's hard for me to believe in miracles. What assurances can I find in the Bible?

The Radical Answer:

If you're looking for miracles . . . you'll find them. If you're not, you won't.

Do You Believe in Miracles?

You are the God who performs miracles; you display your power among the peoples.

Psalm 77:14 NIV

Do you believe that God is at work in the world? And do you also believe that nothing is impossible for Him? If so, then you also believe that God is perfectly capable of doing things that you, as a mere human being with limited vision and limited understanding, would deem to be utterly impossible. And that's precisely what God does.

Since the moment that He created our universe out of nothingness, God has made a habit of doing miraculous things. And He still works miracles today. Expect Him to work miracles in your own life, and then be watchful. With God, absolutely nothing is impossible, including an amazing assortment of miracles that He stands ready, willing, and able to perform for you and yours.

Miracles are not contrary to nature but only contrary to what we know about nature.

St. Augustine

Only God can move mountains, but faith and prayer can move God.

E. M. Bounds

Too many Christians live below the miracle level.

Vance Havner

The impossible is exactly what God does.

Oswald Chambers

A Prayer:

Lord, for You, nothing is impossible. Let me trust in Your power to do the miraculous, and let me trust in Your willingness to work miracles in my life—and in my heart. Amen

What does the Bible say about listening to God?

The Radical Answer:

Prayer is two-way communication with God. Talking to God isn't enough; you should also listen to Him. If you and your family members want to gain a more intimate relationship with God, you should study His Word (every day), worship Him (every day), and talk to Him (many times every day). Remember: The more often you speak to the Creator, the more often He'll speak to you.

Listen Carefully

The one who is from God listens to God's words. This is why you don't listen, because you are not from God.

John 8:47 HCSB

Sometimes God speaks loudly and clearly. More often, He speaks in a quiet voice—and if you are wise, you will be listening carefully when He does. To do so, you must carve out quiet moments each day to study His Word and sense His direction.

Can you quiet yourself long enough to listen to your conscience? Are you attuned to the subtle guidance of your intuition? Are you willing to pray sincerely and then to wait quietly for God's response? Hopefully so. Usually

God refrains from sending His messages on stone tablets or city billboards. More often, He communicates in subtler ways. If you sincerely desire to hear His voice, you must listen carefully, and you must do so in the silent corners of your quiet, willing heart.

In the soul-searching of our lives, we are to stay quiet so we can hear Him say all that He wants to say to us in our hearts.

Charles Swindoll

We cannot experience the fullness of Christ if we do all the expressing. We must allow God to express His love, will, and truth to us.

Gary Smalley

When we come to Jesus stripped of pretensions, with a needy spirit, ready to listen, He meets us at the point of need.

Catherine Marshall

A Prayer:

Lord, give me the wisdom to be a good listener. Help me listen carefully to my family, to my friends, and—most importantly—to You. Amen

What does the Bible say about God's plans for my family and for me?

The Radical Answer:

God has a wonderful plan for you and your loved ones. And the time to start looking for that plan—and living it—is now. Discovering God's plan begins with prayer, but it doesn't end there. You've also got to work at it.

Big Plans

"I say this because I know what I am planning for you," says the Lord. "I have good plans for you, not plans to hurt you. I will give you hope and a good future."

Jeremiah 29:11 NCV

The Bible makes it clear: God has plans—very big plans— for you and your family. But He won't force His plans upon you—if you wish to experience the abundance that God has in store, you must be willing to accept His will and follow His Son.

As Christians, you and your family members should ask yourselves this question: "How closely can we make our plans match God's plans?" The more closely you manage to follow the path that God intends for your lives, the better.

Do you and your loved ones have questions or concerns about the future? Take them to God in prayer. Do you have hopes and expectations? Talk to God about your dreams. Are you and your family members carefully planning for the days and weeks ahead? Consult God as you establish your priorities. Turn every concern over to your Heavenly Father, and sincerely seek His guidance—prayerfully, earnestly, and often. Then, listen for His answers . . . and trust the answers that He gives.

The Almighty does nothing without reason, although the frail mind of man cannot explain the reason.

St. Augustine

Faith never knows where it is being led, but it loves the One who is leading.

Oswald Chambers

A Prayer:

Dear Lord, I will seek Your plan for my life. Even when I don't understand why things happen, I will trust You. Even when I am uncertain of my next step, I will trust You. There are many things that I cannot do, Lord, and there are many things that I cannot understand. But one thing I can do is to trust You always. And I will. Amen

Sometimes, life seems so serious. What should our family do about it?

The Radical Answer:

Learn to laugh at life. Life has a lighter side—look for it, especially when times are tough. Laughter is medicine for the soul, so take your medicine early and often.

So Laugh!

Laugh with your happy friends when they're happy; share tears when they're down.

Romans 12:15 MSG

Laughter is a gift from God, a gift that He intends for us to use. Yet sometimes, because of the inevitable stresses of everyday living, we fail to find the fun in life. When we allow life's inevitable disappointments to cast a pall over our lives and our souls, we do a profound disservice to ourselves and to our loved ones.

If you've allowed the clouds of life to obscure the blessings of life, perhaps you've formed the unfortunate habit of taking things just a little too seriously. If so, it's time to fret a little less and laugh a little more.

So today, look for the humor that most certainly surrounds you—when you do, you'll find it. And remember:

God created laughter for a reason...and Father indeed knows best. So laugh!

I think everybody ought to be a laughing Christian. I'm convinced that there's just one place where there's not any laughter, and that's hell.

Jerry Clower

If you want people to feel comfortable around you, to enjoy being with you, then learn to laugh at yourself and find humor in life's little mishaps.

Dennis Swanberg

There is nothing that rejuvenates the parched, delicate spirits of children faster than when a lighthearted spirit pervades the home and laughter fills its halls.

James Dobson

A Prayer:

Lord, when I begin to take myself or my life too seriously, let me laugh. When I rush from place to place, slow me down, Lord, and let me laugh. Put a smile on my face, Dear Lord, and let me share that smile with all who cross my path . . . and let me laugh. Amen

If I feel guilty about something, what should I do?

The Radical Answer:

First, make sure that you're no longer doing the thing that caused your guilt in the first place. Then, ask for forgiveness (from God and from anybody you've hurt). Next, make sure to forgive yourself. And finally, if you still have residual feelings of bitterness or regret, keep asking God to cleanse your heart. When you ask, He will answer in His own time and in His own way.

Beyond Guilt

There is therefore now no condemnation to those who are in Christ Jesus, who do not walk according to the flesh, but according to the Spirit.

Romans 8:1 NKJV

All of us have made mistakes. Sometimes our failures result from our own shortsightedness. On other occasions, we are swept up in events that are beyond our abilities to control. Under either set of circumstances, we may experience intense feelings of guilt. But God has an answer for the guilt that we feel. That answer, of course, is His forgiveness.

When we ask our Heavenly Father for His forgiveness, He forgives us completely and without reservation. Then, we must do the difficult work of forgiving ourselves in the same way that God has forgiven us: thoroughly and unconditionally.

If you're feeling guilty, then it's time for a special kind of housecleaning—a housecleaning of your mind and your heart . . . beginning NOW!

Identify the sin. Confess it. Turn from it. Avoid it at all costs. Live with a clean, forgiven conscience. Don't dwell on what God has forgotten!

Max Lucado

Prayer is essential when a believer is stuck in the pits of unresolved guilt.

Charles Stanley

Satan wants you to feel guilty. Your heavenly Father wants you to know that you are forgiven.

Warren Wiersbe

A Prayer:

Dear Lord, thank You for the guilt that I feel when I disobey You. Help me confess my wrongdoings, help me accept Your forgiveness, and help me renew my passion to serve You. Amen

I've made plenty of mistakes, and I can't seem to make peace with the past. What should I do?

The Radical Answer:

Everybody makes mistakes—wise people learn from them. And remember that the past is past, so don't live there. If you're focused on the past, change your focus. If you're living in the past, it's time to stop living there (Isaiah 43:18-19).

Beyond the Mistakes

Instead, God has chosen the world's foolish things to shame the wise, and God has chosen the world's weak things to shame the strong.

1 Corinthians 1:27 HCSB

We are imperfect beings living in an imperfect world; mistakes are simply part of the price we pay for being here. Yet, even though mistakes are an inevitable part of life's journey, repeated mistakes should not be. When we commit the inevitable blunders of life, we must correct them, learn from them, and pray for the wisdom to avoid those same mistakes in the future. If we are successful, our missteps become lessons, and our lives become adventures in growth.

Mistakes are the price we pay for being human; repeated mistakes are the price we pay for being stubborn. But, if we are wise enough to learn from our experiences, we continue to mature throughout every stage of life. And that's precisely what God intends for us to do.

Lord, when we are wrong, make us willing to change; and when we are right, make us easy to live with.

Peter Marshall

I hope you don't mind me telling you all this. One can learn only by seeing one's mistakes.

C. S. Lewis

Very few things motivate us to give God our undivided attention like being faced with the negative consequences of our decisions.

Charles Stanley

A Prayer:

Dear Lord, there's a right way to do things and a wrong way to do things. When I do things that are wrong, help me be quick to ask for forgiveness . . . and quick to correct my mistakes. Amen

If I want God to guide me, what should I do?

The Radical Answer:

If you want God's guidance, ask for it. When you pray for guidance, God will give it.

God's Guidance

Every morning he wakes me. He teaches me to listen like a student. The Lord God helps me learn…

Isaiah 50:4-5 NCV

The Bible promises that God will guide you if you let Him. Your job, of course, is to let Him. But sometimes, you will be tempted to do otherwise. Sometimes, you'll be tempted to go along with the crowd; other times, you'll be tempted to do things your way, not God's way. When you feel those temptations, resist them.

What will you allow to guide you through the coming day: your own desires (or, for that matter, the desires of your friends)? Or will you allow God to lead the way? The answer should be obvious. You should let God be your guide. When you entrust your life to Him completely and without reservation, God will give you the strength to meet any challenge, the courage to face any trial, and the wisdom to live in His righteousness. So trust Him today and seek His guidance. When you do, your next step will be the right one.

Fix your eyes upon the Lord! Do it once. Do it daily. Do it constantly. Look at the Lord and keep looking at Him.

Charles Swindoll

God's plan for our guidance is for us to grow gradually in wisdom before we get to the crossroads.

Bill Hybels

We must always invite Jesus to be the navigator of our plans, desires, wills, and emotions, for He is the way, the truth, and the life.

Bill Bright

It is in a prayer relationship that God gives further direction.

Henry Blackaby and Claude King

A Prayer:

Dear Lord, thank You for Your constant presence and Your constant love. I draw near to You this day with the confidence that You are ready to guide me. Help me walk closely with You, Father, and help me share Your Good News with all who cross my path. Amen

Sometimes, I know the thing that needs to be done, but taking action is hard. What should I do?

The Radical Answer:

Pray as if everything depended upon God, and work as if everything depended on you.

Getting It Done Now

When you make a vow to God, don't delay fulfilling it, because He does not delight in fools. Fulfill what you vow.

Ecclesiastes 5:4 HCSB

The old saying is both familiar and true: actions speak louder than words. And as believers, we must beware: our actions should always give credence to the changes that Christ can make in the lives of those who walk with Him.

God calls upon each of us to act in accordance with His will and with respect for His commandments. If we are to be responsible believers, we must realize that it is never enough simply to hear the instructions of God; we must also live by them. And it is never enough to wait idly by while others do God's work here on earth; we, too, must act. Doing God's work is a responsibility that each of us must bear, and when we do, our loving Heavenly Father rewards our efforts with a bountiful harvest.

Do noble things, do not dream them all day long.

Charles Kingsley

Now is the only time worth having because, indeed, it is the only time we have.

C. H. Spurgeon

Every time you refuse to face up to life and its problems, you weaken your character.

E. Stanley Jones

Give to us clear vision that we may know where to stand and what to stand for. Let us not be content to wait and see what will happen, but give us the determination to make the right things happen.

Peter Marshall

A Prayer:

Dear Lord, today is a new day. Help me tackle the important tasks immediately, even if those tasks are unpleasant. Don't let me put off until tomorrow what I should do today. Amen

What does the Bible say about the way I should manage my time? And what about the amount of time I spend with my family?

The Radical Answer:

The Bible warns us that there's no time to waste. Every day—indeed every moment—is precious.

Time for Family

We can't afford to waste a minute, must not squander these precious daylight hours in frivolity and indulgence, in sleeping around and dissipation, in bickering and grabbing everything in sight. Get out of bed and get dressed! Don't loiter and linger, waiting until the very last minute. Dress yourselves in Christ, and be up and about!

Romans 13:13-14 MSG

It takes time to build strong family ties . . . lots of time. Yet we live in a world where time seems to be an ever-shrinking commodity as we rush from place to place with seldom a moment to spare.

Has the busy pace of life robbed you of sufficient time with your loved ones? If so, it's time to fine-tune your priorities. And God can help.

When you make God a full partner in every aspect of your life, He will lead you along the proper path: His path. When you allow God to reign over your life, He will enrich your relationships and your life. So, as you plan for the day ahead, make God's priorities your priorities. When you do, every other priority will have a tendency to fall neatly into place.

I don't buy the cliché that quality time is the most important thing. If you don't have enough quantity, you won't get quality.

Leighton Ford

The more time you give to something, the more you reveal its importance and value to you.

Rick Warren

What really builds togetherness is time spent together—lots of time.

Dennis Swanberg

A Prayer:

Dear Lord, You have given me a wonderful gift: time here on earth. Let me use it wisely—for the glory of Your kingdom and the betterment of my family—today and every day that I live. Amen

It's hard not to be judgmental of other people, and it's hard not to judge their motives. What does the Bible say about judging others?

The Radical Answer:
Your ability to judge others requires a divine insight that you simply don't have. So do everybody (including yourself) a favor: don't judge.

Let God Judge

Stop judging others, and you will not be judged. Stop criticizing others, or it will all come back on you. If you forgive others, you will be forgiven.

Luke 6:37 NLT

We have all fallen short of God's commandments, and He has forgiven us. We, too, must forgive others. And, we must refrain from judging them.

Are you one of those people who finds it easy to judge others? If so, it's time to change.

God does not need (or, for that matter, want) your help. Why? Because God is perfectly capable of judging the human heart . . . while you are not.

As Christians, we are warned that to judge others is to invite fearful consequences: to the extent we judge others, so, too, will we be judged by God. Let us refrain, then, from judging our neighbors. Instead, let us forgive them and love them in the same way that God has forgiven us.

Being critical of others, including God, is one way we try to avoid facing and judging our own sins.

Warren Wiersbe

An individual Christian may see fit to give up all sorts of things for special reasons—marriage, or meat, or beer, or cinema; but the moment he starts saying these things are bad in themselves, or looking down his nose at other people who do use them, he has taken the wrong turn.

C. S. Lewis

Christians think they are prosecuting attorneys or judges, when, in reality, God has called all of us to be witnesses.

Warren Wiersbe

A Prayer:

Dear Lord, sometimes I am quick to judge others. But, You have commanded me not to judge. Keep me mindful, Father, that when I judge others, I am living outside of Your will for my life. You have forgiven me, Lord. Let me forgive others, let me love them, and let me help them . . . without judging them. Amen

This world can be a crazy place. What should I do about the evils that I encounter?

The Radical Answer:

Of course there is darkness in this world, but God's light can overpower any darkness. So make sure that your friend's and family's lives—and faith—are built on the firm foundation of God's Word. Make sure that they have plenty of warning (from you) about the dangers you see them getting too close to. And keep praying that everyone in your family and group of friends will have the wisdom and the strength to avoid the darkness.

On Guard Against Evil

Your love must be real. Hate what is evil, and hold on to what is good.

Romans 12:9 NCV

Nineteenth-century clergyman Edwin Hubbel Chapin warned, "Neutral men are the devil's allies." His words were true then, and they're true now. Neutrality in the face of evil is a sin. Yet all too often, we fail to fight evil, not because we are neutral, but because we are shortsighted: we don't fight the devil because we don't recognize his handiwork.

If we are to recognize evil and fight it, we must pay careful attention. We must pay attention to God's Word, and we must pay attention to the realities of everyday life. When we observe life objectively, and when we do so with eyes and hearts that are attuned to God's Holy Word, we can no longer be neutral believers. And when we are no longer neutral, God rejoices while the devil despairs.

Of two evils, choose neither.

C. H. Spurgeon

God loves you, and He yearns for you to turn away from the path of evil. You need His forgiveness, and you need Him to come into your life and remake you from within.

Billy Graham

God shapes the world by prayer. The more praying there is in the world, the better the world will be, and the mightier will be the forces against evil.

E. M. Bounds

A Prayer:

Lord, strengthen my walk with You. Evil comes in many disguises, and sometimes it is only with Your help that I can recognize right from wrong. Your presence in my life enables me to choose truth and to live a life pleasing to You. May I always live in Your presence. Amen

What does the Bible have to say about the importance of rejoicing?

The Radical Answer:

It's important to rejoice and praise the Father. Joy begins with a choice—the choice to establish a genuine relationship with God and His Son. Joy does not depend upon your circumstances, but upon your relationship with God.

Rejoice Now!

O clap your hands, all peoples; shout to God with the voice of joy.

Psalm 47:1 NASB

Have you made the choice to rejoice? Hopefully so. After all, if you're a believer, you have plenty of reasons to be joyful. Yet sometimes, amid the inevitable hustle and bustle of life, you may lose sight of your blessings as you wrestle with the challenges of everyday life.

Christ made it clear to His followers: He intended that His joy would become their joy. And it still holds true today: Christ intends that His believers share His love with His joy in their hearts.

What does life have in store for you? A world full of possibilities (of course it's up to you to seize them), and

God's promise of abundance (of course it's up to you to accept it). So, as you embark upon the next phase of your journey, remember to celebrate the life that God has given you. Your Creator has blessed you beyond measure. Honor Him with your prayers, your words, your deeds, and your joy.

Joy is the serious business of heaven.

C. S. Lewis

As Catherine of Siena said, "All the way to heaven is heaven." A joyful end requires a joyful means. Bless the Lord.

Eugene Peterson

Some of us seem so anxious about avoiding hell that we forget to celebrate our journey toward heaven.

Philip Yancey

A Prayer:

Dear Lord, You have given me so many blessings; let me celebrate Your gifts. Make me thankful, loving, responsible, and wise. I praise You, Father, for the gift of Your Son and for the priceless gift of salvation. Make me be a joyful Christian and a worthy example to my loved ones, today and every day. Amen

The Bible says I should imitate Christ, but I can never be like Him. So what should I do?

The Radical Answer:

While you can't imitate Christ perfectly, you can follow in His footsteps, you can share His Good News, and you can, to the best of your abilities, obey His commandments. And that's what you should do.

Imitating the Master

Therefore, be imitators of God, as dearly loved children.

Ephesians 5:1 HCSB

Imitating Christ is impossible, but attempting to imitate Him is both possible and advisable. By attempting to imitate Jesus, we seek, to the best of our abilities, to walk in His footsteps. To the extent we succeed in following Him, we receive the spiritual abundance that is the rightful possession of those who love Christ and keep His commandments.

Do you seek God's blessings for the day ahead? Then, to the best of your abilities, imitate His Son. You will fall short, of course. But if your heart is right and your intentions are pure, God will bless your efforts, your day, and your life.

Christlikeness is not produced by imitation, but by inhabitation.

Rick Warren

Every Christian is to become a little Christ. The whole purpose of becoming a Christian is simply nothing else.

C. S. Lewis

A person who gazes and keeps on gazing at Jesus becomes like him in appearance.

E. Stanley Jones

Lord, I am no longer my own, but Yours. Put me to what You will, rank me with whom You will. Let me be employed by You or laid aside for You, exalted for You or brought low by You. Let me have all things, let me have nothing. I freely and heartily yield all things to Your pleasure and disposal. And now, O glorious and blessed God, Father, Son, and Holy Spirit, You are mine and I am Yours. So be it. Amen.

John Wesley

A Prayer:

Dear Jesus, because I am Your disciple, I will trust You, I will obey Your teachings, and I will share Your Good News. You have given me life abundant and life eternal, and I will follow You today and forever. Amen

What does God's Word say about generosity?

The Radical Answer:

The Bible teaches us that generosity is its own reward. So, would you like to be a little happier? Try sharing a few more of the blessings that God has bestowed upon you. In other words, if you want to be happy, be generous. And if you want to be unhappy, be greedy.

The Wisdom to Be Generous

The good person is generous and lends lavishly....

Psalm 112:5 MSG

God's gifts are beyond description, His blessings beyond comprehension. God has been incredibly generous with us, and He rightfully expects us to be generous with others. That's why the thread of generosity is woven into the very fabric of God's teachings.

In the Old Testament, we are told that, "The good person is generous and lends lavishly...." (Psalm 112:5 MSG). And in the New Testament we are instructed, "Freely you have received, freely give" (Matthew 10:8 NKJV). These principles still apply. As we establish priorities for our days and our lives, we are advised to give freely of our time, our possessions, and our love—just as God has given freely to us.

Of course, we can never fully repay God for His gifts, but we can share them with others. And we should.

Nothing is really ours until we share it.

C. S. Lewis

We are never more like God than when we give.

Charles Swindoll

If you want to be truly happy, you won't find it on an endless quest for more stuff. You'll find it in receiving God's generosity and in passing that generosity along.

Bill Hybels

The happiest and most joyful people are those who give money and serve.

Dave Ramsey

A Prayer:

Lord, make me a generous and cheerful giver. Help me to give generously of my time and my possessions as I care for those in need. And, make me a humble giver, Lord, so that all the glory and the praise might be Yours. Amen

Sometimes I have doubts about my future and doubts about my faith. What should I do?

The Radical Answer:

When you have doubts, it is important to take those doubts to the Lord.

When You Have Doubts

An indecisive man is unstable in all his ways.

James 1:8 HCSB

If you're a man who's never had any doubts about his faith, you can stop reading this page now and skip to the next. But if you've ever been plagued by doubts about your faith or your God, keep reading.

Even some of the most faithful Christians are, at times, beset by occasional bouts of discouragement and doubt. But even when we feel far removed from God, God is never far removed from us. He is always with us, always willing to calm the storms of life—always willing to replace our doubts with comfort and assurance.

Whenever you're plagued by doubts, that's precisely the moment you should seek God's presence by genuinely seeking to establish a deeper, more meaningful relationship with His Son. Then you may rest assured that in time,

God will calm your fears, answer your prayers, and restore your confidence.

Doubt may not always be a sign that a man is wrong; it may be a sign that he is thinking.

Oswald Chambers

We basically have two choices to make in dealing with the mysteries of God. We can wrestle with Him or we can rest in Him.

Calvin Miller

Mark it down. God never turns away the honest seeker. Go to God with your questions. You may not find all the answers, but in finding God, you know the One who does.

Max Lucado

A Prayer:

Dear God, sometimes this world can be a puzzling place, filled with uncertainty and doubt. When I am unsure of my next step, keep me mindful that You are always near and that You can overcome any challenge. Give me faith, Father, and let me remember always that with Your love and Your power, I can live courageously and faithfully today and every day. Amen

What does the Bible say about love?

The Radical Answer:

God is love, and He expects you to share His love with others.

A Father's Love

This is my command: Love one another the way I loved you. This is the very best way to love. Put your life on the line for your friends.

Genuine love requires patience and perseverance. Sometimes we are sorely tempted to treat love as if it were a sprint (which it is not). Genuine love is always a marathon, and those who expect it to be otherwise will always be disappointed.

Building lasting relationships requires a steadfast determination to endure, and as an example of perfect perseverance, we need look no further than our Savior, Jesus Christ. Jesus finished what He began. Despite the torture He endured, despite the shame of the cross, Jesus was steadfast in His faithfulness to God. We, too, must remain faithful in our relationships, especially during times of transition or hardship.

The next time you are tempted to "give up" on a relationship, ask yourself this question: "What would our Savior do?" When you find the answer to that question, you will know precisely what you should do.

Christian love, either towards God or towards man, is an affair of the will.

C. S. Lewis

Homes that are built on anything other than love are bound to crumble.

Billy Graham

Joy is love exalted; peace is love in repose; gentleness is love in society; goodness is love in action; faith is love on the battlefield; meekness is love in school; and temperance is love in training.

D. L. Moody

A Prayer:

Lord, You have given me the gift of love and You've asked me to share it. The gift of love is a precious gift indeed. Let me nurture love and treasure it. And, help me remember that the essence of love is not to receive it, but to give it, today and forever. Amen

What does the Bible say about eternal life?

The Radical Answer:

God offers you a priceless gift: the gift of eternal life. If you have not already done so, accept God's gift today—tomorrow may be too late.

The Gift of Eternal Life

Just then someone came up and asked Him, "Teacher, what good must I do to have eternal life?" "Why do you ask Me about what is good?" He said to him. "There is only One who is good. If you want to enter into life, keep the commandments."

Matthew 19:16-17 HCSB

Your ability to envision the future, like your life here on earth, is limited. God's vision, however, is not burdened by any such limitations. He sees all things, He knows all things, and His plans for you extend throughout eternity.

God's plans are not limited to the events of daily life. Your Heavenly Father has bigger things in mind for you . . . much bigger things. So praise the Creator for the gift of eternal life and share the Good News with all who cross your path. And remember: if you have given your heart to the Son, you belong to the Father—today, tomorrow, and for all eternity.

Someday you will read in the papers that Moody is dead. Don't you believe a word of it. At that moment I shall be more alive than I am now. I was born of the flesh in 1837, I was born of the spirit in 1855. That which is born of the flesh may die. That which is born of the Spirit shall live forever.

D. L. Moody

Teach us to set our hopes on heaven, to hold firmly to the promise of eternal life, so that we can withstand the struggles and storms of this world.

Max Lucado

Once a man is united to God, how could he not live forever? Once a man is separated from God, what can he do but wither and die?

C. S. Lewis

A Prayer:

Lord, I am only here on this earth for a brief while. But, You have offered me the priceless gift of eternal life through Your Son Jesus. I accept Your gift, Lord, with thanksgiving and praise. Let me share the good news of my salvation with those who need Your healing touch. Amen

Sometimes it's hard to be hopeful. What does the Bible say about hope?

The Radical Answer:

Don't give up hope. Other people have experienced the same kind of hard times you may be experiencing now. They made it, and so can you (Psalm 146:5).

Finding Hope

This hope we have as an anchor of the soul, a hope both sure and steadfast.

Hebrews 6:19 NASB

Are you a hope-filled man? You should be. After all, God is good; His love endures; and He has offered you the priceless gift of eternal life.

But sometimes hope slips away, even for the most optimistic people. Despite God's promises, despite Christ's love, and despite our countless blessings, we can still fall prey to discouragement and doubt. When we do, we need the encouragement of fellow believers, the life-changing power of prayer, and the healing truth of God's Holy Word.

If you find yourself falling into the spiritual traps of worry and discouragement, seek the healing touch of Jesus and the encouraging words of fellow Christians. If you find a friend in need, remind him or her of the peace that is found through a personal relationship with Christ. This world can be a place of trials and tribulations, but as believers, we are secure. God has promised us peace, joy, and eternal life. And, of course, God keeps His promises today, tomorrow, and forever.

Faith looks back and draws courage; hope looks ahead and keeps desire alive.

John Eldredge

If your hopes are being disappointed just now, it means that they are being purified.

Oswald Chambers

The hope we have in Jesus is the anchor for the soul—something sure and steadfast, preventing drifting or giving way, lowered to the depth of God's love.

Franklin Graham

A Prayer:

Today, Dear Lord, I will live in hope. If I become discouraged, I will turn to You. If I grow weary, I will seek strength in You. In every aspect of my life, I will trust You. You are my Father, Lord, and I place my hope and my faith in You. Amen

Sometimes the truth hurts. What does the Bible say about integrity?

The Radical Answer:

The Bible leaves no room for doubt: Total honesty is the only path for those who seek to follow Christ. Truth sets you free; untruth imprisons you. So measure your words accordingly.

The Best Policy

Better to be poor and honest than a rich person no one can trust.

Proverbs 19:1 MSG

It has been said on many occasions and in many ways that honesty is the best policy. For believers, it is far more important to note that honesty is God's policy. And if we are to be servants worthy of Jesus Christ, we must be honest and forthright in our communications with others. Sometimes, honesty is difficult; sometimes, honesty is painful; sometimes, honesty is inconvenient; but always honesty is God's commandment.

In the Book of Proverbs, we read, "The Lord detests lying lips, but he delights in men who are truthful" (12:22 NIV). Clearly, we must strive to be men whose words are pleasing to our Creator. Truth is God's way, and it must be our way, too, even when telling the truth is difficult. As loving fathers, we can do no less.

God doesn't expect you to be perfect, but he does insist on complete honesty.

Rick Warren

A little lie is like a little pregnancy. It doesn't take long before everyone knows.

C. S. Lewis

Maintaining your integrity in a world of sham is no small accomplishment.

Wayne Oates

A Prayer:

Heavenly Father, You instruct Your children to seek truth and to live righteously. Help me always to live according to Your commandments. Sometimes, Lord, speaking the truth is difficult, but let me always speak truthfully and forthrightly. And, let me walk righteously and courageously so that others might see Your grace reflected in my words and my deeds. Amen

I've developed some bad habits. What should I do?

The Radical Answer:

Target your most unhealthy habit first, and attack it with vigor. When it comes to defeating harmful habitual behaviors, you'll need focus, determination, prayer, more focus, more determination, and more prayer.

Healthy Habits

Do not be deceived: "Evil company corrupts good habits."

1 Corinthians 15:33 NKJV

It's an old saying and a true one: First, you make your habits, and then your habits make you. Some habits will inevitably bring you closer to God; other habits will lead you away from the path He has chosen for you. If you sincerely desire to improve your spiritual health, you must honestly examine the habits that make up the fabric of your day. And you must abandon those habits that are displeasing to God.

If you trust God, and if you keep asking for His help, He can transform your life. If you sincerely ask Him to help you, the same God who created the universe will help you defeat the harmful habits that have heretofore defeated you. So, if at first you don't succeed, keep praying. God is listening, and He's ready to help you become a better person if you ask Him . . . so ask today.

You will never change your life until you change something you do daily.

John Maxwell

The simple fact is that if we sow a lifestyle that is in direct disobedience to God's reveled Word, we ultimately reap disaster.

Charles Swindoll

Since behaviors become habits, make them work with you and not against you.

E. Stanley Jones

Prayer is a habit. Worship is a habit. Kindness is a habit. And if you want to please God, you'd better make sure that these habits are your habits.

Marie T. Freeman

A Prayer:

Dear Lord, help me break bad habits and form good ones. And let my actions be pleasing to You, today and every day. Amen

Sundays have become very busy around our house. Our schedules are full, and we hardly have time to slow down long enough to catch our breath. In the future, how should we reorganize our Sundays?

The Radical Answer:

The Sabbath is unlike any other day. Your job is to observe the Sabbath, not ignore it.

Observing the Sabbath

Remember the Sabbath day, to keep it holy.

Exodus 20:8 NKJV

When God gave Moses the Ten Commandments, it became perfectly clear that our Heavenly Father intends for us to make the Sabbath a holy day, a day for worship, for contemplation, for fellowship, and for rest. Yet we live in a seven-day-a-week world, a world that all too often treats Sunday as a regular workday.

How does your family observe the Lord's day? When church is over, do you treat Sunday like any other day of the week? If so, it's time to think long and hard about your family's schedule and your family's priorities.

Whenever we ignore God's commandments, we pay a price. So if you've been treating Sunday as just another day, it's time to break that habit. When Sunday rolls around, don't try to fill every spare moment. Take time to rest . . . Father's orders!

Worship is not taught from the pulpit. It must be learned in the heart.

Jim Elliot

Worship is a daunting task. Each worships differently. But each should worship.

Max Lucado

There is no division into sacred and secular; it is all one great, glorious life.

Oswald Chambers

God has promised to give you all of eternity. The least you can do is give Him one day a week in return.

Marie T. Freeman

A Prayer:

Dear Lord, I thank You for the Sabbath day, a day when my family and I can worship You and praise Your Son. We will keep the Sabbath as a holy day, a day when we can honor You. Amen

How does the Bible instruct me to direct my thoughts?

The Radical Answer:

Watch what you think: If your inner voice is, in reality, your inner critic, you need to tone down the criticism now. And while you're at it, train yourself to begin thinking thoughts that are more rational, more accepting, and less judgmental.

The Direction of Your Thoughts

Finally brothers, whatever is true, whatever is honorable, whatever is just, whatever is pure, whatever is lovely, whatever is commendable—if there is any moral excellence and if there is any praise—dwell on these things.

Philippians 4:8 HCSB

Thoughts are intensely powerful things. Our thoughts have the power to lift us up or drag us down; they have the power to energize us or deplete us, to inspire us to greater accomplishments or to make those accomplishments impossible.

How will you and your family members direct your thoughts today? Will you obey the words of Philippians 4:8 by dwelling upon those things that are honorable, true, and worthy of praise? Or will you allow your thoughts to be hijacked by the negativity that seems to dominate our troubled world?

Are you fearful, angry, bored, or worried? Are you so preoccupied with the concerns of this day that you fail to thank God for the promise of eternity? Are you confused, bitter, or pessimistic? If so, God wants to have a little talk with you.

God intends that you experience joy and abundance, but He will not force His joy upon you; you must claim it for yourself. It's up to you and your loved ones to celebrate the life that God has given you by focusing your minds upon "whatever is commendable." So form the habit of spending more time thinking about your blessings and less time fretting about your hardships. Then, take time to thank the Giver of all things good for gifts that are, in truth, far too numerous to count.

It is the thoughts and intents of the heart that shape a person's life.

John Eldredge

A Prayer:

Dear Lord, I will focus on Your love, Your promises, and Your Son. When I am weak, I will turn to You for strength. When I am troubled, I will turn to You for patience and perspective. Help me guard my thoughts, Lord, so that I may honor You this day and forever. Amen

Sometimes I'm impatient for life to unfold. What does the Bible say about God's timing?

The Radical Answer:

God has very big plans in store for your life, so trust Him and wait patiently for those plans to unfold. And remember: God's timing is best, so don't allow yourself to become discouraged if things don't work out exactly as you wish. Instead of worrying about your future, entrust it to God. He knows exactly what you need and exactly when you need it.

God's Timetable

He has made everything beautiful in its time. He has also set eternity in the hearts of men; yet they cannot fathom what God has done from beginning to end.

Ecclesiastes 3:11 NIV

Are you anxious for God to work out His plan for your life? Who isn't? As believers, we all want God to do great things for us and through us, and we want Him to do those things now. But sometimes, God has other plans. Sometimes, God's timetable does not coincide with our own. It's worth noting, however, that God's timetable is always perfect.

The next time you find your patience tested to the limit, remember that the world unfolds according to God's plan, not ours. Sometimes, we must wait patiently, and that's as it should be. After all, think how patient God has been with us.

God has a designated time when his promise will be fulfilled and the prayer will be answered.

Jim Cymbala

God is in no hurry. Compared to the works of mankind, He is extremely deliberate. God is not a slave to the human clock.

Charles Swindoll

The stops of a good man are ordered by the Lord as well as his steps.

George Mueller

A Prayer:

Dear Lord, Your wisdom is infinite, and the timing of Your Heavenly plan is perfect. You have a plan for my life that is grander than I can imagine. When I am impatient, remind me that You are never early or late. You are always on time, Father, so let me trust in You. Amen

What does the Bible say about discipleship?

The Radical Answer:
God's Word instructs you to follow in Christ's footsteps. And when it comes to discipleship, you owe it, not just to yourself or to God, but also to your family to be a devoted follower of the One from Galilee.

The Decision to Be His Disciple

He has showed you, O man, what is good. And what does the LORD require of you? To act justly and to love mercy and to walk humbly with your God.

Micah 6:8 NIV

When Jesus addressed His disciples, He warned that each one must, "take up his cross and follow Me." The disciples must have known exactly what the Master meant. In Jesus' day, prisoners were forced to carry their own crosses to the location where they would be put to death. Thus, Christ's message was clear: in order to follow Him, Christ's disciples must deny themselves and, instead, trust Him completely. Nothing has changed since then.

If we are to be disciples of Christ, we must trust Him and place Him at the very center of our beings. Jesus never comes "next." He is always first. The paradox, of course, is that only by sacrificing ourselves to Him do we gain salvation for ourselves.

Do you seek to be a worthy disciple of Christ? Then pick up His cross today and every day that you live. When you do, He will bless you now and forever.

As we seek to become disciples of Jesus Christ, we should never forget that the word disciple is directly related to the word discipline. To be a disciple of the Lord Jesus Christ is to know his discipline.

Dennis Swanberg

There is not Christianity without a cross, for you cannot be a disciple of Jesus without taking up your cross.

Henry Blackaby

A disciple is a follower of Christ. That means you take on His priorities as your own. His agenda becomes your agenda. His mission becomes your mission.

Charles Stanley

A Prayer:

Help me, Lord, to understand what cross I am to bear this day. Give me the strength and the courage to carry that cross along the path of Your choosing so that I may be a worthy disciple of Your Son. Amen

I want to become a wiser, more thoughtful person. Where can I go to find wisdom?

The Radical Answer:

If you own a Bible, you have ready access to God's wisdom. Your job is to read, to understand, and to apply His teachings to your life . . . starting now and ending never.

Wisdom Now!

Do you want to be counted wise, to build a reputation for wisdom? Here's what you do: Live well, live wisely, live humbly. It's the way you live, not the way you talk, that counts.

James 3:13 MSG

The great English preacher, Charles Haddon Spurgeon, once wrote, "Wisdom is the right use of knowledge. To know is not to be wise. Many men know a great deal, and are all the greater fools for it. But to know how to use knowledge is to have wisdom." Spurgeon was, indeed, a very wise man.

To become wise, we must seek God's wisdom and live according to His Word. And, we must not only learn the lessons of the Christian life, we must also live by them.

Do you seek to live a life of righteousness and wisdom? If so, you must study the ultimate source of wisdom:

the Word of God. You must seek out worthy mentors and listen carefully to their advice. You must associate, day in and day out, with godly men and women. And, you must act in accordance with your beliefs. When you do these things, you will become wise . . . and you will be a blessing to your friends, to your family, and to the world.

The more wisdom enters our hearts, the more we will be able to trust our hearts in difficult situations.

John Eldredge

If you lack knowledge, go to school. If you lack wisdom, get on your knees.

Vance Havner

Knowledge is horizontal. Wisdom is vertical; it comes down from above.

Billy Graham

A Prayer:

Dear Lord, give me wisdom to love my family, to care for them, and to help them understand the wisdom of Your Holy Word. Let me share Your wisdom by the words I speak and the example that I set, today and every day that I live. Amen

What promises does God's Word make about salvation?

The Radical Answer:

God offers you life abundant and life eternal. Accept God's salvation through Jesus Christ and begin to live.

For God So Loved the World

This is how much God loved the world: He gave his Son, his one and only Son. And this is why: so that no one need be destroyed; by believing in him anyone can have a whole and lasting life.

John 3:16 MSG

Christ sacrificed His life on the cross so that we might have eternal life. This gift, freely given by God's only begotten Son, is the priceless possession of everyone who accepts Him as Lord and Savior. God is waiting patiently for each of us to accept the gift of eternal life. Let us claim Christ's gift today.

It is by God's grace that we have been saved, through faith. We are saved not because of our good deeds but because of our faith in Christ. May we, who have been given so much, praise our Savior for the gift of salvation, and may we share the joyous news of our Master's love and His grace.

God did everything necessary to provide for our forgiveness by sacrificing His perfect, holy Son as the atoning substitute for our sins.

Franklin Graham

The way to be saved is not to delay, but to come and take.

D. L. Moody

The essence of salvation is an about-face from self-centeredness to God-centeredness.

Henry Blackaby

There is no detour to holiness. Jesus came to the resurrection through the cross, not around it.

Leighton Ford

A Prayer:

Dear Lord, I am only here on this earth for a brief while. But, You have offered me the priceless gift of eternal life through Your Son Jesus. I accept Your gift, Lord, with thanksgiving and praise. Let me share the Good News of my salvation with all those who need Your healing touch. Amen

Index of Topics

1.	God First	8	28. Celebration	62
2.	Blessings	10	29. Optimism	64
3.	Strength	12	30. Worry	66
4.	Daily Devotional	14	31. Dreams	68
5.	Righteousness	16	32. Joy	70
6.	Future	18	33. Teaching Discipline	72
7.	Purpose	20	34. Forgiveness	74
8.	Life	22	35. Enthusiasm	76
9.	Choices	24	36. Leadership	78
10.	Failure	26	37. Talents	80
11.	Patience	28	38. Focus	82
12.	Example	30	39. Conscience	84
13.	Kindness	32	40. Perseverance	86
14.	Silence	34	41. Anger	88
15.	Adversity	36	42. Prayer	90
16.	Faith	38	43. God's Strength	92
17.	Service	40	44. Christ's Sacrifice	94
18.	Discipline	42	45. Praise	96
19.	Encouragement	44	46. Sin	98
20.	Thanksgiving	46	47. God's Love	100
21.	Work	48	48. Fear	102
22.	Acceptance	50	49. Learning	104
23.	Courage	52	50. Problems	106
24.	God's Word	54	51. Negativity	108
25.	Grace	56	52. Beliefs	110
26.	Materialism	58	53. Fearing God	112
27.	Following Christ	60	54. God's Calling	114

55.	Attitude	116	82.	Time with Family	170
56.	Worship	118	83.	Judging Others	172
57.	Fitness	120	84.	Evil	174
58.	Contentment	122	85.	Rejoicing	176
59.	Repentance	124	86.	Imitating Christ	178
60.	Busyness	126	87.	Generosity	180
61.	Jesus	128	88.	Doubts	182
62.	Obedience	130	89.	Love	184
63.	Family	132	90.	Eternal Life	186
64.	Testimony	134	91.	Hope	188
65.	Humility	136	92.	Integrity	190
66.	God's Promises	138	93.	Habits	192
67.	Peace	140	94.	Sabbath	194
68.	God's Presence	142	95.	Thoughts	196
69.	Golden Rule	144	96.	God's Timing	198
70.	Fun	146	97.	Discipleship	200
71.	Happiness	148	98.	Wisdom	202
72.	Self-confidence	150	99.	Salvation	204
73.	God's Protection	152			
74.	Miracles	154			
75.	Listening to God	156			
76.	God's Plans	158			
77.	Laughter	160			
78.	Guilt	162			
79.	Mistakes	164			
80.	God's Guidance	166			
81.	Action	168			